Escape the Expected

Tom Trush
P.O. Box 7141
Phoenix, AZ 85011
Phone: 602.305.6755
E-mail: tom@writewaysolutions.com
Website: http://www.writewaysolutions.com

Editors: Linda Sandow and Ken Darrow, M.A.

Cover design by Andy Renk

First Printing: August 2014

ISBN: 1500266795
ISBN-13: 9781500266790

Escape the Expected

The Secret Psychology of Selling to Today's Skeptical Consumers

by
Tom Trush

Praise for 'Escape the Expected'

"Tom Trush has hit another home run with his new book **Escape the Expected: The Secret Psychology of Selling to Today's Skeptical Consumers.** From business owners and sales directors to agency heads and marketing consultants, Tom shows you how to cut through the clutter, clamor and chaos in today's marketplace of confusion.

"When you test a few of the secrets in Tom's new guidebook, you'll quickly see that this isn't just another rehash of marketing principles. Instead, it's the key you've been looking for that helps you succeed so you can work less, spend more time with your family, and let your marketing program to do the heavy lifting.

"Really, can one book do all that? Yes, this one can."

Trey Ryder
The Ryder Method™ of Education-Based Marketing

"Trust Trush on trust! Tom Trush hits the nail on the head with his new book, **Escape the Expected.** People don't trust marketing messages anymore. They must contain elements they can trust, which is a tough these days with all of the half-cocked messages pummeling our senses. Tom takes us through a trilogy of practical ways to introduce and leverage trust in our marketing messages.

"Tom's 30-day challenge gives excellent advice to target a single marketing improvement area, determine what is holding you back, find someone who has successfully tackled the same problem and then model their success for 30 days. Well done, Tom!"

Paul D. Guyon
TheUltimateMastermindGroup.com

"Tom Trush has penned an undeniably timely book of strategies for getting ahead in THE most important competitive advantage of the 21st century: trust."

Charles E. Gaudet II
Author of *The Predictable Profits Playbook*

"Direct, hard-hitting and authentic are the best words to describe what Tom has done with his new book. Getting attention and trust are the two biggest challenges facing all marketers. Tom has nailed it with this book! He shares effective ways to build trust and connect with others faster and with better results. Get this book now."

Tony Rubleski
#1 Bestselling Author, Speaker and Consultant

"Wow! My intention was to read a few lines of Tom Trush's *Escape the Expected* before I went to bed early. I kept taking notes and brainstorming new ideas. I finished the book in one evening. I stayed up even later and started implementing his principles. I love the short, to-the-point chapters. I am updating my website and will be applying the knowledge he gifted me."

Wendy Schweifler
Goddess of Health, BOD-E-NOMICS, LLC
Co-author, *Your Body is Your Business and YOU are the CEO!*

"If you're fed up with 'monkey see, monkey do' marketing, Tom's third book, *Escape the Expected,* will really rattle your cage. Your customers are bombarded every day with thousands of messages – all fighting for attention. Tom has uncovered the deceptively simple, secret strategy all marketers need to cut through the clutter and win more business – TRUST.

"What I love about Tom's book is that it's practical and actionable. I have a list of new ideas that I'll plug in to my business this month. If you're looking to grow your business the right way, by building trust first, grab this book and check out now!"

Andy Renk
AndyRenk.com

Table of Contents

TRUST TRILOGY PART III:
Your marketing must develop relationships
before it can drive profits.

Foreword

Tom Trush knows that all successful selling has one factor in common:

Trust.

Whether you're an executive negotiating a big contract or a teenager trying to mow lawns for money (as I did in my youth), exchanges are always easier when you quickly establish trust. The belief in a person's reliability and honesty is the foundation for effective communication.

So how then do you establish trust when marketing your product or service?

That's the question Tom Trush tackles and conquers in *Escape the Expected*.

Too often we view prospects/consumers as mindless individuals who only require a perfect sales pitch to transform them into eager buyers. As a result, many sales and marketing folks focus on finding "secret words" or shortcuts to generate sales.

But, as Tom Trush clearly explains in this powerful book, you need only to prove that you share a common goal and an identical desire to achieve it. I call it "Sales Infiltration."

Fortunately, you were a customer long before you became an entrepreneur/executive/business owner. You understand how people like to be treated in selling situations.

Now you simply have to put your own desires aside and apply your prospects' preferences to your promotional efforts.

At times, Tom's concepts seem stunningly simple – and they are. You won't find a tip, strategy or idea in this book that you can't implement today – usually with minimal effort!

From discoveries made in university laboratories, grocery store aisles and even the shores of a desert fishing pond, Tom shares insights and stories that can transform you into one of your industry's most trusted resources.

If your business is to thrive in today's information-overloaded age, learning how to establish trust when marketing is an absolute must.

What you're about to discover in Tom Trush's *Escape the Expected* may very well change your entire approach to sales and marketing for the better – and it certainly has the capacity to boost your bottom line.

Here's to your success!

Ben Gay III
Salesman/Sales Trainer
The Closers
www.bfg3.com

Introduction

No doubt, you trust people you know more than strangers. But ever notice how some strangers quickly close the trust gap? Even though you just met them or were introduced to their product or service, you instantly feel a sense of trust.

We all experience these situations.

So why does this reaction happen? And, more importantly, how can you create this response so people sense the same belief in you (and your products or services)?

Well, let me start off by giving you an idea to consider.

When researching trust in marketing for this book, one factor kept coming up in situations where trust gets established fast. Over and over, it seems you can shortcut the trust process by tapping a powerful emotion ...

Surprise.

Simply put, go beyond what's expected and trust often follows. Even better if your surprise demonstrates that you both share a common goal.

Let's look at kids' restaurant preferences as an example. The instant children enter the world, a mysterious power permeates their minds, causing them to shout "McDonald's" every time you ask "Where do you want to eat?"

It's hard to understand the appeal of crappy burgers and processed chicken nuggets. However, study the situation from a child's perspective and you understand the attraction.

You see, McDonald's doesn't just offer food – it creates experiences. There are the play areas ... cartoonish characters like Ronald McDonald ... product tie-ins to popular movies ... and even a surprise toy inside each Happy Meal.

All these items combine to create an experience that goes beyond the usual food served at home or other restaurants.

Ever order shoes from Zappos? If so, I bet you received them before the promised delivery date.

The unexpected surprise likely left you with strong feelings for the company.

Fly Virgin Airlines? I guarantee your eyes were glued to the preflight safety video. (If you haven't seen the unexpected surprise, watch it here: http://youtu.be/DtyfiPlHslg.)

Research shows our brains are hard-wired to gain pleasure from unexpected events. In fact, this desire is so strong that some scientists believe surprises and drugs have similar addictive effects on our brains.

So What Does the Trustworthy Marketing Look Like?

Unfortunately, many business owners, entrepreneurs and executives are trapped. They believe marketing must look, feel and function a certain way.

So when they create their "marketing," the end result appears pretty standard.

You see logos ... company names ... lists of services ... product images ... phone numbers ... URLs ... staff and/or office pictures ...

This mentality is dangerous because your prospects sense the look, feel and function of marketing too. And when they perceive something as marketing, they often ignore it.

Most do so instinctively. Like you, people have programmed their minds to tune out information that targets a mass audience with an impersonal message.

The fact is, each day thousands more messages compete for people's attention than just a decade ago. Thanks to the Internet, it's possible this figure may even reach into the millions.

What's more, anyone can now create and distribute information at minimal or no cost, which adds clutter to an already crowded marketplace. That's why it's essential you escape the expected with your marketing.

Again, marketing that matches an expected look and feel goes unnoticed.

The mind doesn't wait. You literally have fractions of a second to demonstrate differences – whether through appearance or content – when marketing.

In January 2014, research released by a team of MIT neuroscientists found that the human brain processes entire images in as little as 13 milliseconds (1 millisecond is 1/1,000th of a second).

"The fact that you can do that at these high speeds indicates to us that what vision does is find concepts," said Mary Potter, an MIT professor of brain and cognitive sciences and the study's senior author. *"That's what the brain is doing all day long – trying to understand what we're looking at."*

So how fast is 13 milliseconds?

Well, the average blink of an eye takes 300-400 milliseconds. That's an eternity when compared to the time the mind needs to process images.

Time is not on your side.

So as you read this book, keep questioning your prospects' expectations. Then begin to brainstorm ways you can use your marketing to deliver the unexpected.

I kept each chapter short. That way it's easier for you to implement ideas without feeling overwhelmed with excess information.

Read from cover to cover, or pick chapters that relate to your marketing challenges. Whatever way you decide, I wish you the best of success.

Tom Trush

TRUST TRILOGY
PART I:

Instead of marketing what you want to say, give prospects what they need to succeed.

Chapter 1

Are You Prepared for This Frightening Fact?

Trust among Americans keeps dropping. In fact, according to an Associated Press-GfK poll released in November 2013, a weakening belief in people has continued for the past four decades.

Only one-third of Americans say most people can be trusted (half the respondents in 1972 felt the same way). Amazingly, a related study put this lack-of-trust figure at a whopping 83%.

Toss in the supposed shady dealings within the business community – as believed by many in the general public – and you can understand why we're at a disadvantage when pitching prospects.

Generating sales without trust is nearly impossible. Trust drives consumers' buying decisions today. So incorporating trust elements into your marketing is absolutely critical.

Unfortunately, as more companies get desperate for sales, it's crazy how trust and honesty become less of a priority.

For proof, look at banks. Overdraft charges have become a major revenue source. And little is done to warn customers when balances reach low levels because their mistakes bring in big bucks.

According to a recent study detailed by ABC News, overdraft fees at U.S. banks range from $8-$45 per transaction. During the last fiscal year, checking account overdraft fee revenue increased to $31.5 billion – a $700 million increase over the previous fiscal year.

Seems many banks could establish much-needed trust by simply letting customers know when balances get low.

What do you think?

Shortly after the first Gulf War in 1991, the insurance company USAA refunded car insurance premiums paid by thousands of members stationed in the Middle East. Since the men and women were serving, the company thought it was unfair to charge the premiums.

After all, their cars were most likely sitting unused inside U.S. garages.

Surprisingly, many refund checks went uncashed. Nearly 2,500 were sent back to USAA by grateful customers who told the company to keep the money and just be there "when we need you."

Imagine you worked for another U.S. insurance company. Would you have any chance convincing USAA's customers who received refund checks to do business with you?

Of course not.

A simple, trustworthy action by USAA likely led to a lifetime of loyalty.

We live in a time where a surplus of information creates increased interaction. As described in Don Peppers and Martha Rogers' book, *Extreme Trust: Honesty as a Competitive Advantage*, we are "a dynamic and robust network of electronically interconnected people in a worldwide, 24/7 bazaar of creating and sharing, collaborating, publishing, critiquing, helping, learning, competing, and having fun."

Messages move fast and that speed keeps getting quicker.

Moore's Law is the observation that computers get about a thousand times more powerful every 15-20 years. This also carries over to our interaction with people. Technological progress has led to quicker and more convenient ways to communicate with anyone anywhere.

How are you using these advancements to your advantage?
Peppers and Rogers predict …

"Technology has now changed the landscape of competition so much that a new, more extreme form of trustworthiness will be required in order to be successful. Simply doing what you say

you're going to do and charging customers what you say you're going to charge them will no longer be sufficient.

"Instead, businesses will be expected to protect the interest of their customers proactively – to go out of their way, to commit resources, and to use their insights and expertise in such a way as to help customers avoid making mistakes or acting against their own interest simply through their own oversight."

The message is clear: If you keep following a "traditional" branding approach when marketing, your business' future is in danger.

Chapter 2

The Diminishing Desire
Your Prospects Crave

T rust has always been critical to business success. Penalties for not having it are severe – loss of credibility, value and, of course, sales. After all, no one wants to do business with someone who isn't trustworthy, right?

On the other hand, providing products and services in a trustworthy manner brings big benefits. Interactions increase, credibility rises and your reputation grows.

Especially now, consumers crave relationships with companies they can trust. They're fatigued by the stress caused by today's economic environment. They've seen scams pulled by banks, credit card companies, insurance carriers and many others.

The problem, however, is most marketing doesn't demonstrate the trust consumers desire. Instead, companies push self-serving information that ignores prospects' needs.

Again, rapid technology development has increased our interaction with others. You have more ways than ever to get in front of people. As a result, you have more opportunities to attract prospects' attention – but that doesn't mean you have their interest. (You may want to read that sentence again.)

Those who establish trust are the ones who get heard.

So you can understand why so many sales-first marketing messages get as much attention as a white crayon in a Crayola box, especially when they represent the initial contact with prospects.

You see, trust when marketing isn't demonstrated by just adding a testimonial or two, highlighting awards or even doing what you say you're going to do.

Technology has changed the competitive landscape so much that a more extreme form of trustworthiness is needed.

Today's prospects expect you to proactively protect their interests. They expect you to dedicate resources to them before pitching your product/service. They expect you to use your insights and expertise to help them avoid mistakes. They expect you to put their well-being before your profits.

Whether fair or not, this is the reality.

Chapter 3

The Wrong Way to Sell Your Products and Services

U nfortunately, a dangerous epidemic continues to surge through the business community, especially among professionals selling services. In fact, the problem is so prevalent that I gave it a name – *The Juswanem Syndrome*.

Sounds a bit odd, doesn't it?

I'll explain what it means in minute. But first, let's set the scene ...

As I often stress, those who don't consistently market their services often find themselves in frustrating situations. Time and again, the need for sales leads them to the first marketing opportunity that comes to mind.

These days that activity usually involves social media. Resources such as Twitter, Facebook and LinkedIn remain the shiny objects offering promises of almost endless prospects.

And rightfully so – social media is an incredible connection tool.

The problem, though, is the approach.

You see, regardless of tool, resource, strategy or tactic, service providers often express to me a similar desired action from prospects. And it almost always begins with the same words:

I just want them. (Or, as the quicker spoken version sounds, *I "juswanem."*)

The full request might sound like:

I juswanem to call me. If I just get prospects on the phone, I know I can convince them to do business with me.

Unfortunately, this approach is one of the quickest ways to turn off potential buyers. After all, who does it benefit?

YOU!

The Juswanem Syndrome leads to marketing messages that show prospects lack of respect. It causes you to protect the information prospects seek. This barrier then pushes prospects elsewhere to find the initial guidance they crave.

Instead of a phone call, why not first focus on establishing trust? A positive belief in you is critical when attracting prospects and turning them into your clients. Without trust, you have zero chance at generating a sale.

Now, let's look at the three primary reasons we trust people ...

1. **Previous Behavior:** Past behavior is usually a strong predictor of future actions.

2. **Capability:** We trust people based on what we believe they can do.

3. **Alignment:** If we share a common goal, then there's a strong chance we'll work together to get there.

Of these three reasons, alignment is the most important (yet most ignored) when marketing.

Today, more than ever, you must prove you're not just someone pushing services.

Unfortunately, in most marketing situations, the alignment between buyers and sellers matches as well as oil and water. After all, your goal is to make sales. Whereas a prospect simply wants to solve a problem.

Chapter 4

Why People Don't Trust You (and How to Fix the Problem)

E ver notice how you trust some people almost instantly? Why does this happen? And why do we label people in certain industries as untrustworthy, even though we never met them?

The answer, at least according to a recent study by Jacobs University researchers, comes down to inequality – especially with income.

After analyzing data from a 30-country survey on quality of life, researchers discovered inequality lowers interpersonal trust and boosts the fear of not being well-respected by other people.

As you know, lack of trust is common within the business community (and, as you read in the introduction, the problem keeps getting worse). Many prospects enter buying/hiring situations fearing they'll get taken advantage of.

In some cases, income differences play a role. But based on the Jacobs study, knowledge inequality can also trigger distrust.

For example, let's look at legal services. Most lawyers are honest professionals who want to help their clients. So why does a "can you trust your lawyer" Google search bring up 51.5 million results?

Worse yet, why does the same search for doctors reveal a whopping 100 million results?

Success in these professions requires education and knowledge that most people don't have. Furthermore, many individuals deem doctors and lawyers as high-earning professions.

These factors combine to create a distrust double whammy!

So how can you establish trust in your marketing when your prospects sense inequality, whether in income or knowledge?

Showing empathy is a strong starting point. Prove to prospects you understand what they're feeling. Use their language and show you both operate on the same level.

If you only pitch your products or services, you demonstrate little concern for your prospects' situation.

Keep in mind, marketing offers an opportunity to tell stories that your audience can relate to. So share case studies or explain how you helped someone overcome a challenge (preferably one your prospects are experiencing right now).

For generations, people have used stories to emotionally engage and share information. This evolutionary trait works to your advantage.

Of course, you also want to share your knowledge. Few actions create trust faster than unexpected help.

Chapter 5

Why Today's Consumers Create Fewer Leads

As the person responsible for marketing and generating leads for your company, you face serious challenges today.

After all, have you ever stopped to consider how easy it is for prospects to find your competitors?

Today, more than ever, new and shifting technologies have made it effortless for prospects to find alternatives to your product or service. What's more, this competitive marketplace spans all industries and grows bigger every day.

Making your situation more challenging are consumers' increasingly stubborn expectations and demands.

If you've experienced a slowdown in leads, today's well-informed prospect is one place where you can pinpoint your problem.

It's no longer enough to "exceed expectations," "deliver excellent service," "offer customer-focused solutions," or "have an experienced team." Today's prospects demand you deliver value before they even consider doing business with you.

Few companies have adjusted their marketing to accommodate today's consumers – and that leaves incredible opportunity for you.

Search online, open the newspaper, scan your mailbox, flip through the *Yellow Pages* or read a few emails. You'll see little difference in marketing approaches.

Not only do pushing products and slinging services remain the norm, but the same words get used over and over again.

So what's the solution?

Well, one way you can differentiate yourself in marketing is to make your prospects feel important.

Let me explain ...

Think back to the last time you met someone who made you feel special. The type of person who you instantly enjoyed being around. Someone who could spark a smile from just about anybody.

How did that person act when you met? What did he/she talk about? Who received most of the attention?

Most likely, that person made you feel important (and good about yourself) because the conversation centered around you.

Right?

Now consider how this approach carries over to marketing.

You see, most attention in marketing focuses on hyping a company or its product/services. I often compare this approach to the person at a party who only talks about himself, laughs at his own jokes and always has a story that tops whatever anyone else says.

People cringe when this person walks into a room. So imagine how your prospects feel when they see this same "strategy" used in your marketing.

If you want to generate more leads, shine the spotlight away from your company. Stop thinking about what you can get from your marketing and instead focus on what you can give.

Chapter 6

How Today's Marketing Shift Changes Your Responsibilities

We're standing in the trenches of a marketing revolution. Greater consumer demands ... changing technology ... more messages ... different strategies ... new metrics ...

These changes combine to create added challenges for anyone responsible for generating leads.

The competitive marketplace grows larger every day, meaning alternatives to your product or service are as close as a mouse click.

Unfortunately, few companies make adjustments to accommodate today's informed consumer. This inflexibility presents big problems.

You see, if your marketing tells prospects what they need instead of providing for their needs, it's time to rethink your approach.

Just as the way people interact with the world has changed, so has their method for gathering information. Patience is not a priority for today's prospects.

Not long ago, businesses held an advantage because they controlled the availability of information. Gathering insight into a product or service required traveling to a store, talking to a salesperson, picking up the phone or watching/reading an ad that delivered a controlled message.

These days, almost everyone turns to the Internet to satisfy an ever-increasing appetite for information. As a result, prospects now own the advantage.

They expect access to information in different formats – and they want it now. When your marketing doesn't meet these needs, you get ignored.

But here's the good news:

Besides their hunger for information, today's prospects are on a continuous quest to find something worth sharing. They seek to distribute activities, opinions and media that entertain or inform.

In fact, even topics typically unworthy of interest get shared. Spend just a few seconds on Facebook, Twitter, YouTube or any other social network, and you see personal posts published only as a ploy for attention.

Please understand, though, this is not a knock against social media. I believe it's an incredibly effective tool for making connections and spreading your message.

After all, social media use exploded because it exploits an evolutionary trait hardwired into our brains. The human race survives and thrives by sharing experiences.

So what motivates people to share your marketing?

Chapter 7

The Easiest Way to Add Trust to Your Marketing Copy

A crazy transformation happens when many business owners and entrepreneurs sit down to write marketing copy.

It's as if an invisible force commands control of their bodies. Their mentality shifts ... judgment escapes ... and the hype machine revs into high gear.

What results is self-absorbed copy that reeks of aggressive propaganda. A large portion reads like outlandish B.S., while the remaining words push a forceful sell.

To avoid this problem, I suggest an exercise that stumps even the most well-meaning business owners and entrepreneurs. If you're up for the following challenge, I'm certain you'll see rewards for your efforts.

Take a piece of paper and write down five reasons for contacting your prospects and current clients ... but your purpose can't involve pitching your product or service.

Ready ... go!

Did you hear that little voice inside your head? I bet it questioned the logic behind this exercise.

After all, isn't the goal of being in business to generate sales? Isn't that the reason you contact prospects and clients?

I'd argue no – not always.

Of course, contacting prospects and clients *only* to pitch your product or service might get you occasional sales. But it does little to develop a relationship – an essential factor when it comes to long-term sales, repeat buyers and referrals.

You see, trust is the most common element missing from marketing copy. Sales pitches and (most) advertising are low on the trust scale, while relationship building and collaboration represent the new standard in "selling."

Widely available and inexpensive tools for interacting with people have created new ways of creating value with prospects and clients. Companies experiencing marketing success these days use educational material to first build a trust foundation. The people behind these brands create and distribute content that, instead of pitching, triggers interaction.

Think about this concept for a minute …

When you write marketing copy, you start with a blank document – a virtual piece of paper that's worthless. However, as you add words, the value increases based on the knowledge you share. The more you reveal, the greater the value.

In effect, you're no different than an artist who starts with a blank canvas. **Your words are the "paint" that determines what prospects are willing to pay for your product or service.**

You have the power to create unlimited value for your prospects. So don't hesitate to give away some of your best tips, tricks and techniques.

Now let's get into a few examples ...

You may not expect it; however, the U.S. Postal Service does an excellent job educating prospects about how to effectively use direct mail. The resource the federal agency uses is *Deliver* magazine.

Go to www.delivermagazine.com and you'll see heaps of how-to information. According to the USPS ...

- 43% of *Deliver* readers say it has increased their intention to spend more on direct marketing.

- 67% of readers say it has increased their opinion of direct marketing.

- More than 50% have taken action in the last year as a result of *Deliver* articles.

- There have been more than 70,000 downloads from the DeliverMagazine.com website, including more than 3,130 white papers.

Not too shabby, right?

Paint company Sherwin-Williams uses a similar medium with its *STIR Magazine*. The online publication targets an audience that includes interior designers, architects and people passionate about home decorating.

During a recent visit, I saw articles explaining how to complete an ego-friendly, sustainable kitchen makeover; how to pick colors for commercial and residential environments; and ways you can use red to evoke responses. Videos offered behind-the-scenes access to TV production and commercial designers.

What's also noticeable is the frequent interactivity between visitors and *STIR* team members.

When it comes to shopping, you may know Whole Foods as a high-end grocery store. But don't overlook the copy the company uses to promote its products. Scroll to the bottom of the grocer's website home page and you'll see guides to main courses, baking and holiday recipes.

Of course, if you need the suggested ingredients, you can quickly find them stocked on the supermarket's shelves.

Think that's a coincidence? No way!

Other interactive items include a servings calculator, a guide for wine pairing and a company blog.

You can see how educational copy establishes trust in all these examples. What results is a well-informed audience that becomes more motivated to buy. The process takes patience, but the returns are long-lasting.

Remember, today's competitive landscape means a more extreme form of trustworthiness is needed. Prospects expect you to

proactively protect their interests ... they expect you to dedicate resources to them ... they expect you to use your insights and expertise
to help them avoid mistakes ... and they expect you to put their well-
being before your profits.

Whether fair or not, this is the reality.

Chapter 8

Have Prospects Who Don't Respond After an Inquiry? Try This ...

A recent Northwestern University study that examined doctors' visits with patients revealed insight that can affect how prospects perceive you during an initial interaction.

But before I share the details, I must warn you ...

Don't discount the simplicity of what you're about to read or assume the concept won't work in your industry.

The study, published in the *Journal of Participatory Medicine*, analyzed doctors' first-time interactions with patients suffering from common colds. The doctors used paper charts (computerized systems were removed so attention could focus on nonverbal cues) and spent about 3.5 minutes with each patient.

Following the visits, each patient was asked questions to help measure their perception of their doctor's empathy and likeability, as well as the "connectedness" they felt toward their doctor.

Researchers then analyzed the video recordings second-by-second, paying close attention to nonverbal communication. They concluded that, while social touch and visit length can play a role in a patient's perception of empathy, one factor was the most critical to establishing trust ...

Eye contact.

This simple action, researchers stressed, can lead to patients who return for care, adhere to medical advice and stay with the same providers.

Makes sense, doesn't it? After all, eye contact shows you're focused and paying attention. It also indicates openness in communication.

But here's the problem for us:

As professional service providers, many times our first communication with prospects isn't face-to-face. So we can't make eye contact. As a result, we miss opportunities to establish instant trust.

For instance, let's say someone submits an inquiry through your website or emails you about your services. What do you do?

Typically, you might reply with an email that introduces yourself, answers any questions and provides an offer to further assist.

Right?

Prospects who submit inquiries online expect these types of responses – and that's fine. Many companies follow this approach.

But what I recommend to my clients (especially those with too many prospects who don't respond/engage after an initial inquiry) is to reply back with a video message. Simply record a quick video that addresses your prospect's inquiry and introduces yourself.

Keep in mind, your prospects don't expect to see a video ... your face and eye contact ... or a personalized message. All these factors work to your advantage.

This about this for a minute ...

When you see someone for the first time, you instantly create an impression. Your intuition tells you if you like that person or sense a bad feeling. Whether positive or negative, these first impressions last.

So how do you feel about people who go beyond what's expected to help you?

Of course you remember these people. You hold them in higher regard. You look for ways to return the favor.

Fortunately, you achieve this status every time you go beyond your prospects' expectations. Your first interaction is just the starting point.

NOTE: Screencast-O-Matic (http://www.screencast-o-matic.com) is one way to record prospect videos fast. With the push of a button, you can record a screencast video for free (while also using your webcam) and share a link that plays your message.

Chapter 9

Have You Fallen Victim to The Differentiation Myth?

S ometimes advice gets shared so often that people assume it's fact without giving it a second thought.

Let me explain ...

I was hired by a mortgage banker to improve an underperforming radio ad campaign. During my initial conversation with the client, I asked for recordings of all the current ads.

So he sent a request to the radio station. Within a couple hours, I had the ads and an email with advice for my client from the station's ad rep.

Here's a portion of that email:

For copy points, I'd really like to see commercials that are much more personalized for your company and your business – why should I shop with your company and why should I work with (client's name removed)? What separates you from the competition?

This wording may sound familiar. After all, "what separates you from the competition" and "why should I shop with your company" are common phrases preached by marketing professionals for decades.

They're also part of a dangerous myth that far too many business owners and entrepreneurs fall victim to.

You see, differentiation is not the reason prospects decide to do business with you.

Now I know I'll get flack for making this claim. But before you shoot down my notion (because it doesn't match the marketing norm), hear me out ...

Yes, differentiation is important. In fact, I often stress the need to "dare to be different." But relying on differentiation as the solution that gets prospects to take action on your offer is foolish.

Think back to the last time someone asked what made you different. In my client's case, one differentiating factor is experience. Few mortgage bankers in his area have as much time in the mortgage game as him.

In fact, he heavily promoted this detail in previous radio ads. However, the claim did little to set him apart from anyone in his industry. After all, how often do people stress experience in their marketing?

All the time, right?

Instead of differences, I recommend you concentrate on establishing trust in your marketing. Trust is critical when attracting prospects and turning them into clients. Without trust, you have zero chance at generating a sale.

So let's again dig into the three primary reasons we trust people:

1. **Previous Behavior:** Past behavior is usually a strong predictor of future actions.

2. **Capability:** We trust people based on what we believe they can do. For example, I trust my mechanic to fix my car because I'm aware of his past training/experience.

3. **Alignment:** If we share a common goal, then I trust we'll work together to get there.

Of these three reasons, again, alignment is the most important (yet most ignored) when marketing. Prospects could't care less about your sales goals.

So, to create an alignment, you must match your marketing to your prospects' problems.

Here's one example of how I tackled this task using a 60-second radio spot (name/contact info changed for privacy):

Attention Arizona Residents Who Went Through a Short Sale or Foreclosure:

If you want to buy a home again, you're likely confused about your requirements for getting another mortgage. After all, with so much misinformation floating around, how do you know what to believe?

Steve Smith's latest special report, **The New Mortgage and Refinance Rules for Arizona Homeowners***, explains what you need to know to protect your finances and get a money-saving mortgage after a short sale or foreclosure.*

Get your free guide today at www.xyzmortgage.com or call 602-555-5555.

You'll discover ...

- *The real truth about when you can buy again,*

- *How to make yourself more appealing to lenders,*

- *What credit changes you must make now to prove you can manage your money,*

- *And much more.*

Get **The New Mortgage and Refinance Rules for Arizona Homeowners** *today at www.xyzmortgage.com or call 602-555-5555. Again, that's xyzmortgage.com or call 602-555-5555. Get your free report now.*

Notice how the message is 100% focused on delivering information that helps prospects solve problems. You don't see a pitch mentioning experience, years in business, academic degrees or even a company name.

Instead, the entire message revolves around prospects' needs. The added benefit is the ad positions my client as an industry authority – not just another mortgage broker begging for business.

The offer also allows prospects to gather information without human interaction. That way we eliminate prospects' fear of getting pitched.

So if you were in the target market (i.e., someone who went through a short sale or foreclosure and now wants to buy a home), would this ad pique your interest?

Chapter 10

How Selfish Selling Pollutes the Marketing World

I n most buying situations, you think about yourself and what you want.

Right?

Of course, there's nothing wrong with this mentality – it's perfectly normal. In fact, I'd argue you can't effectively take care of others if you don't first take care of yourself.

Problems arise, however, when you carry over the "me-first" mentality into marketing. **Unless you understand what others want, you'll have a difficult time selling anything, especially in print.**

When writing a marketing piece, thinking about your needs first creates an instant disconnect.

From the opening word to the final punctuation mark, you must focus on how to help your prospects ... how your offer benefits them ... how your product/service makes their lives easier ... and why their lives will be better with what you offer (and more difficult without it).

In order to effectively communicate these items, replace your desires with sensitivity to your prospects' needs.

You see, marketing through print is a way to share knowledge with the world. Many business owners and entrepreneurs go about the process the wrong way, though.

They see today's marketing tools, such as the Internet, e-mail and social media, as quick communication vehicles. So they blast pitch-heavy messages over and over again with little regard for who sees them (unless, of course, a recipient is willing to pull out a wallet).

The result is marketing pollution.

If your marketing doesn't provide value, you're just adding contamination to an already tainted marketplace.

Take a look at your last marketing piece and ask yourself ...

- Did I give away information that helped prospects learn something new?

- Did I answer at least one common question?

- Did I help prospects solve a problem by sharing ideas?

- Did I strive to create a relationship, not just a quick sale?

- Did I provide information so compelling that prospects would want to share it with their networks?

Or did you distribute the marketing piece because ...

- You knew "you should be marketing?"

- You hoped it would generate leads to boost your lagging sales?

- You thought you should post something for social media?

Put meaningful marketing out to the world and you'll be rewarded with responses.

Chapter 11

Are You Marketing for Failure?

"**F**ailure only happens when you stop trying."

No doubt, you've seen a version of this quote before. I bring it up again because I'm often reminded of how well the advice applies to marketing.

So often, business owners and entrepreneurs seek out the magic pill to marketing nirvana. They crave the secret to a single action that results in an instant stream of leads.

One action … one marketing medium … one shot at opportunity …

Well, the truth is this approach rarely returns results, especially when you're desperate for revenue.

You see, business owners and entrepreneurs who aren't consistent marketers frequently need leads fast because revenue dries up. So they put all their efforts into one approach. When it doesn't work, they give up and stop marketing altogether.

This is like the baseball player who steps up to the plate, swings and misses at the first pitch, and then stubbornly stands with his bat stuck on his shoulder. Of course, a hit in this situation can't happen.

Just like in baseball, you must keep swinging when marketing, regardless of what happens on your first attempts. Marketing is a process you refine over time. And let's be honest …

No one gets it right the first time around.

Effective marketing is an evolving process – the amount of change depends on how much work you put forth.

So are you willing to keep swinging?

Here are several tips to help you the next time you step up to the plate:

- The most important piece of the promotional puzzle is attention-grabbing, compelling copy that delivers value.

- You can't create effective marketing if you rely on interrupting as many people as possible with a message they never asked for.

- Listen to your prospects' most pressing problems, fears, frustrations, desires and dreams – then use those words to craft your messages.

- Instead of just talking about your product or service, explain to prospects what it will do for them.

And one final thought …

When you compare your marketing efforts against results achieved by others, you will always fail – at least in your mind. You come up short every time you determine your success by others' accomplishments.

Chapter 12

The 7 Responsibilities of
an Ad That Sells

On the bottom shelf next to my desk sits (for easy access) what is arguably the most comprehensive course ever written on advertising – *How to Convert White Space Into Advertising That Sells*.

It was developed by Clyde Bedell, the first person recorded in the National Retail Advertising Hall of Fame.

Written in 1940, Bedell's course consists of 15 manuals and a 536-page hardcover book. Each page is crammed with content, ads and stories, including this one ...

A Bedell student was moving from Minnesota to California for a new newspaper job. The student didn't want to drive the long distance, so he ran the following classified ad:

Owner wants car driven to California. Will pay all the driver's expenses.

He then sat back and waited for responses to roll in. But after 24 hours, nothing. The same after 48 hours ... and even 72 hours later.

Confused and frustrated, he thought through Bedell's ad writing process. Then, suddenly, he realized the problem.

So he went back, changed the ad and re-ran it. Within 24 hours, he had 28 responses. Three days later, that number jumped to 63.

Amazingly, the student only changed a single word.

So what was it?

He replaced "car" with "Cadillac."

The two words offer enormous differences. Driving a clunker cross country offers little appeal (which is what readers likely envisioned the first time). However, sitting at the controls of a Cadillac is appealing to many.

The response increase illustrates the power of specific words over vague or general terminology. Even a single word has immense power in copy.

Throughout his teachings, it's clear Bedell had one basic belief when writing ads:

All good selling is serving.

He was also adamant about running ads for a purpose. According to Bedell, the 7-fold responsibility of every ad is ...

(1) to attract

(2) and hold

(3) the favorable attention

(4) of the maximum economic number

(5) of the right kind of people (prospects)

(6) while a selling story is told

(7) and a desired action or reaction is induced.

"Don't be content with ads that make statements and convey value," he wrote. "Make it your aim to induce action through your ads ... If you are preoccupied with being creative, making a pretty ad, impressing your fellow ad men, you are an unworthy ad person. Your job is to make people want something and to get them to do something about it."

Chapter 13

How to Prove Your Capabilities Without Sounding Like an 'Expert'

How often do see words such as "expert," "skilled," "professional," or "knowledgeable" used in marketing materials?

Especially among service providers, these terms show up everywhere – and understandably so. They give a glimpse into your capabilities.

But using these words creates a problem. Prospects see them so often that the language loses its effect. Being an "expert" or "professional" turns into just another common claim shared by others in your industry.

So how can you prove your skill and deepen desire for your product or service without sounding like everyone else?

Well, I suggest applying what I call *The Kid Creation Effect*. Let me share a short story to explain how it works …

One Saturday morning, I walked into the kitchen to find my 5-year-old son making breakfast. This sight isn't unusual for the want-to-be chef; Alex loves coming up with new kitchen creations.

This time he had frozen waffles, a loaf of a bread and syrup. First, he toasted two waffles and tossed them on his plate. Then he grabbed a slice of untoasted bread and placed it between the waffles. The stack was then slathered with syrup.

Alex sat at the table and devoured his breakfast with barely a breath.

No doubt, this situation would have been different if I created the same meal for him.

"What's this bread doing between my waffles?" he would have asked while giving a confused look at his plate.

You see, kids have difficulty finding fault with just about anything they create or discover alone. And, not so surprisingly, adults often share this characteristic.

So, instead of forcing an idea/thought/fact on your prospects, gain an advantage by helping them come to conclusions on their own.

Self-tests work well for these situations. You simply walk prospects through questions that prove your knowledge, present a problem and help identify solutions related to your product or service.

You may have seen the self-test Christopher Chabris and Daniel Simons used to demonstrate selective attention and promote their book, *The Invisible Gorilla: How Our Intuitions Deceive Us.* (Look up "invisible gorilla" on YouTube.)

During the so-called "invisible gorilla" you watch two groups of people – some dressed in white, some in black – pass around basketballs. You're asked to count how many times the players dressed in white pass the ball.

For most people, focusing on the passing ball causes them to become blind to the unexpected. In this case, they (me included) fail to see the gorilla passing through the scene.

Dr. Mehmet Oz, an excellent marketer, uses self-tests all the time. For example, a search on his site for food allergies reveals a Food Allergy Symptom Checker. You simply go through the test to discover if you have allergies that require a doctor visit.

When Orabrush needed to promote a new tongue cleaner, it did so by creating an educational video that explained how to tell when your breath stinks. As of this writing, the *Bad Breath Test – How to Tell When Your Breath Stinks* video on YouTube has nearly 19 million views.

Remember, helping prospects come to a conclusion makes your marketing message memorable. But just another claim only makes it the same.

Chapter 14

Are These Wasted Words Damaging Your Marketing Message?

"*EXCEEDING EXPECTATIONS*"

The new banner splashed across a self-storage facility's sign caused me to groan in disgust.

I first saw the phrase from the road. Then I pulled into the gas station next door to get a closer look. Unfortunately, the wasted words continued on the other side of the sign ...

"We're almost full. Come see why."

Are you kidding me? Does the owner of the storage facility really believe these types of phrases attract customers? Are they even truthful?

You don't need me to remind you that every inch of a marketing piece (or, in this case, a sign) is precious real estate. Which is why I can't understand the reason behind using meaningless words, large logos and insignificant pictures – instead of copy that drives action and delivers value.

Here are a few more of my favorite wasted words:

Value added ... leading provider ... full service ... innovative ... commitment to clients ... leverage ... cost effective ... next generation ... wide range of solutions ... flexibility ... world class ... premier ... cutting edge ... mission critical ... groundbreaking ... advanced ... proactive approach ...

Little searching is needed, especially online, to find these phrases within marketing messages. In fact, search any service-related industry in Google and I bet you find one of these words within 30 seconds.

What's crazy is few people would ever think to use wasted words in a conversation. For example, let's say we just met and I ask what you do. Would you respond by saying:

I'm a leading innovative solutions provider who delivers a complete range of cost-effective products and services designed to meet the ever-increasing needs of my clients.

Of course not!

Now, other wasted words aren't as obvious as the above examples. They do, however, deliver just as much damage to your marketing message.

One quick way to find them is simply through logic. **You see, many people and companies over-promote characteristics they should have or actions they're supposed to do.**

For instance, in a recent blog post, I talked about a chiropractor's website that promised "to improve quality of life by facilitating healing in a compassionate, caring and friendly environment."

Can you imagine the alternative?

I also mentioned a worker's compensation attorney who markets himself as being "experienced," "dedicated to fighting for your rights" and "committed to getting you the compensation you deserve."

As a prospect, you already expect these traits, right? So why waste space promoting them?

It's easy for business owners and entrepreneurs to fall back on words others use to describe the benefits of becoming a client/customer. This is also why you must stay away from using them in your marketing message.

Every day your prospects subconsciously tune out most marketing messages, while giving attention to a select few. The messages rewarded with interest have distinctive differences or target a desire your prospects are actively thinking about.

For proof, think about your daily activities. If you noticed every marketing message competing for your attention, you'd go insane (and that's not an exaggeration). Fortunately, your mind filters out the unnecessary interruptions.

When you copy competitors' marketing ideas, you create repetitive images in your prospects' minds. You disregard the brain's biologically programmed preference for differences. And, as a result, your message drowns in a sea of sameness.

Now, let's go back to that storage facility banner again ...

Search Google for a phrase such as "how to pick a storage unit" and you'll see roughly 18 million results. Topics range from selecting the right size unit and indentifying the appropriate security to evaluating vehicle access and benefits of climate-controlled facilities.

Judging by the search results, prospects feel confused when searching for storage units. So it only makes sense to use your marketing to clear up all the misunderstanding.

Imagine you were looking for storage unit and saw the following banner:

Don't fall for the tricks that cause you to overpay for a storage unit and put your property at risk. Come inside or visit www.smithselfstorage.com today for your FREE storage awareness guide!

Would this get your attention?

I bet it would. Furthermore, this offer helps establish the facility (and the people who work there) as a trusted resource – instead of just another place pitching storage space.

Keep in mind, consumers crave information they can believe. They've been exposed to so much aggressive hype, promises and pitches from so-called experts that they're naturally skeptical of self-serving promotion.

The bottom line: Your words won't persuade if they don't deliver value.

Chapter 15

How to Use Questions and Commands to Create Conversational Copy

You'd think writing conversational copy would be easy. After all, you just use the words and phrases you and your prospects speak every day.

Simple, right?

Well, the problem is most people don't write the way they talk. Instead, they turn to the formal tone taught by high school English teachers. The result is a stiff, boring style that isn't easy to read or remember.

Copy that connects with prospects is conversational. When read aloud, it sounds like you're talking to a friend over lunch.

You have short words (and sentences) … repeated information … occasional questions … and causal pauses …

You also engage one person – not a large audience. And the dialog goes back and forth.

Of course, if you haven't used this type of copy in your marketing before, it might seem odd at first. You'll likely feel uncomfortable even trying to write it.

Don't worry, though. Your natural voice will eventually come through after a little practice. If you continue having trouble, record yourself telling someone about your product or service. Then transcribe the recording.

One easy way I trigger mental dialogue in copy is with one- or two-word questions. I write a statement and then give the reader an opportunity to pause and take in the idea.

Some of my favorite questions include "Make sense?" "Right?" "Understand?" "Fair enough?" and "Sound familiar?"

Have a look at the questions in this example:

You're fed up with searching for strategies and finding time to act on them. You're sick of seeing your inbox pummeled with pitches for products promising improbable profits.

What you'd rather have is someone to stand by your side, walk you through the marketing process, and show you what steps to take next.

Right?

Or, what you need is a sounding board for critical marketing decisions. You want the security that comes with picking up your phone, calling a trusted advisor and asking, "Is this the right move?" or "Can you look this over and tell me what you think?"

Sound familiar?

Now I realize the guidance people want varies from business to business. So now you can get my expertise at any level you need – and without a long-term commitment.

Another conversational copy technique is inserting command statements at the beginning of sentences. Some of my favorites are "listen," "remember," "keep in mind" and "imagine."

For instance …

Keep in mind, when you don't grab control of your 401k or at least educate yourself about your investment options, you limit your retirement to what the market delivers.

You can also use longer command statements as transitions. Here are several examples:

Allow me to explain …
Listen to this story …
Let's take a look at what I'm talking about …
Think about that for a minute …
And here's one fact you can't ignore …

WARNING: Yes, you should use proper punctuation and spelling. But writing conversationally means sometimes breaking the "rules." So don't be surprised if your copy sometimes causes grammarians to break out in cold sweats.

You can occasionally use one-sentence paragraphs (even one-word paragraphs) … start a sentence with "and" or "but" … include sentence fragments … and even create contractions.

These grammar violations help match your marketing copy with the way your prospects speak, which, in turn, makes your message more memorable.

Chapter 16

Double Your Odds of a 'Yes' Response With This Technique

O ver the years, I've shared many techniques for persuading prospects in your marketing materials.

Some simpler ones include the "because" approach to controlling your prospects' actions, the mind-manipulating word that can create buyers, and how to demonstrate similarities that trigger action.

Well, now I have something new for your bag of persuasion tricks. But unlike the techniques mentioned above, I'm still testing this one.

You see, I just saw it in a recent *Inc.* magazine article. Still I believe the technique is worth sharing because it's so easy to incorporate into your marketing. What grabbed my attention is how the technique is supported by 42 studies on 22,000 people.

The concept is simple: Use words that reaffirm people's freedom of choice.

In marketing situations, this choice is often whether to buy or not. So you remind prospects that they have the right to decline your offer.

Across all 42 studies, a "yes" response was twice as likely when an offer was followed by a reminder that a "no" response was okay, too.

This approach is known as the "But You Are Free" technique. In addition to the BYAF phrase, another one that worked just as well during studies was "but, obviously, do not feel obliged."

As you can see, the exact words aren't important – only that prospects know they control the decision.

And here's a catch …

The best results were achieved in face-to-face situations.

Studies showed, however, that writing the words (especially through e-mail) work when persuading prospects, too.

Chapter 17

Why Trying to Beat Your Competition is Risky

"**W**hat if working like crazy to beat the competition did exactly the opposite – made you mediocre and more like the competition?" Harvard Business School professor Youngme Moon poses this thought on the back cover of her book, *Different: Escaping the Competitive Herd*.

The question is worthy of attention, especially in today's business world where "we're different" claims are as common as coffee at Starbucks. **After all, difference isn't a characteristic you can just talk about; you must prove it.**

But how can you? How do you get prospects to differentiate your offerings from your competitors?

Well, if you're in an industry where your service (or product) isn't part of a regular shopping experience and prospects have many options, you have a tough task.

Here's a quick example that explains why;

Until about age 13, I collected baseball cards. My dad lived behind a shopping mall, so my twin brother and I would spend our allowances on Topps wax packs at the nearby drug store.

Every year we created checklists so we could match our new cards with what we needed to create a complete set. The cards were then organized in albums and boxes.

We would also read *Beckett Baseball Card Monthly* like a minister studies the Bible. That way we always knew what our cards were worth (which was helpful when trading with friends).

In many cases, we could rattle off a card's value by just giving it a quick glance.

But while we understood what differences made baseball cards valuable, our parents had no clue and wondered why we kept wasting our money. They saw each card as the same – a rectangular piece of stiff paper with a picture on the front and statistics on the back.

Prospects have similar reactions when shopping for a new service or product. **As Moon describes in her book, "Where a connoisseur sees the differences, a novice sees the similarities."**

When you're familiar with an industry, you can deconstruct your decisions. You make choices based on factors that you know are important.

But when you're unfamiliar with an industry, you don't have this luxury. You don't know the differentiating factors. And, as a result, most offerings look the same.

This is one reason why creating educational content for your prospects is so critical to an effective marketing strategy. Remember, most prospects prefer information – not instant sales pitches.

When you only push services and showcase your company, you become just another fish in a sea of sameness.

Chapter 18

Is 'Getting the Word Out' Really Worth Your Effort?

B usiness development experts often encourage "getting the word out" about your company as a way to drive sales.

The theory is, as the number of people who know about your business grows, so will your profits.

But is this marketing-to-the-masses approach really worth the effort?

I'm not so certain.

You see, simply making people aware of your company's products or services does <u>not</u> trigger action (or a buying response), especially when marketing.

Think about it …

Are you interested in every sight or sound that attracts your attention?

Of course not.

Here in Phoenix, we recently had city council elections. So candidates' signs littered just about every street corner. You couldn't help but see them each time you stopped at an intersection.

As a result, I could tell you every person running for the seat in my district. The signs told me the names, but did nothing to spark further interest.

Keep in mind, awareness also does <u>not</u> generate desire, which (again) is critical to marketing that leads to sales.

How often have you met someone and, within seconds, had a business card forced in your face and a request to "do business"?

You see this tactic all the time at networking events. But hey, aren't these people "getting the word out"?

In these instances, awareness can actually diminish desire.

The reality is that reaching people with your message is not hard. What's difficult is getting prospects to pay attention to your marketing, find value in your message and then take an action that eventually leads to sales.

Traditional branding or image marketing relies on consistently reminding people what you offer.

In effect, this is marketing to the masses – and most marketing and advertising falls into this category. (Think big brands such as Nike, Pepsi, Microsoft, Apple, etc.) The process is time-consuming and extremely expensive.

The smarter approach, especially for smaller businesses, is using your marketing to target specific prospects – and then persuading them to take a measurable action (e.g., request information, visit a web page, download a report, send an email, etc.). The people who respond then become leads worthy of greater marketing attention and effort.

So which would you rather have: name awareness or leads?

Chapter 19

Use This Motivator to Boost Response on Your Marketing

D rive down Jefferson Street here in downtown Phoenix on a summer evening and you'll likely see snack vendors outside Chase Field, home of the Arizona Diamondbacks.

Most set up shop with just a table, umbrella and a couple of coolers.

They strategically position themselves to catch fans entering the ballpark. You see, the vendors sell many of the same snacks you find at the concession stands inside. The only difference?

Outside, the prices are much cheaper – and the vendors repeatedly remind you.

So you might hear a pitch like ...

THIRSTY?! Grab your bottle of water here for only $1. Wait until you get inside and you'll pay $3.

Please note that final sentence.

Now, let's say you need to write a marketing piece to announce your product.

How do you go about the process?

If you think strategically, you begin by brainstorming your product's benefits. You then figure out what pain your product solves and come up with a motivating offer that addresses this problem and gets prospects to act.

Seem similar to your approach?

If so, congratulations. Your actions go beyond what the typical entrepreneur or executive does when writing marketing copy.

However, you may be overlooking a critical motivator ...

The fear of loss.

The fact is, to achieve the best response, you must explain what prospects lose by not taking action on your offer. Remind them that their pain and problems continue if they don't get your solution right now. (Review the above vendor pitch again.)

Let's look at a couple examples ...

GOOD: Contact us today to perform your Envoys upgrade. We'll make sure you get access to new functionality and your database remains supported by Envoys.

BETTER: Contact us today to perform your Envoys upgrade. We'll make sure you get access to new functionality and your database remains supported by Envoys.

Keep in mind, if you don't upgrade before April 30, you'll need to shell out hefty support fees just to maintain access to your database. Furthermore, the longer you wait, the higher the probability that you face a complicated upgrade or re-implementation process – which can increase your costs even more. Call us now at 555.555.5555.

GOOD: Click here to try the next three issues of *The Business Owner's Tax Savings Report* for free. You'll get simple tax-saving tips and discover how to save on real estate, insurance, car repairs and more.

BETTER: Click here to try the next three issues of *The Business Owner's Tax Savings Report* for free. You'll get simple tax-saving tips and discover how to save on real estate, insurance, car repairs and more.

Without these strategies, you're almost certain to overspend on taxes this year. What's more, you put yourself at greater risk for paying penalties – even if you hire a conservative accountant and don't take a single "questionable" deduction. Download your first issue now.

So remember, remind prospects what they'll lose and you'll gain more responses.

Chapter 20

Would You Respond to Your Current Marketing?

You've heard the saying before ...

People do business with people they know, like and trust.

During the marketing process, this concept especially rings true. The challenge you face, though, is that your first introduction to someone often isn't in person. So your marketing materials – in just a few seconds – must begin to establish these feelings in your prospects' minds.

So how can you overcome this challenge?

Well, the first step is to understand what causes people to respond to marketing. The fact is ...

People take action on your marketing for their own reasons – not yours.

Sure, this statement might seem like common sense. But it's worth stressing because the concept rarely gets enough consideration when business owners and entrepreneurs develop marketing materials.

Your reasons for marketing are to gather leads and generate sales. These objectives don't match your prospects' needs. All they want are solutions to their problems.

So instead of marketing your business, products or services, share information that targets your prospects' desires.

Understand the difference?

If you sell air conditioners and target homeowners with old units, you might give your prospects the warnings signs that occur before a cooling system breaks down. After all, most homeowners want to keep their families comfortable and avoid costly repairs, right?

If you sell auto insurance and target drivers who overpay for coverage, you might share strategies for securing discounts and cutting costs.

You make yourself known, likeable and trustworthy when you give prospects information they can immediately use. You also create interest in your marketing, which attracts new prospects.

Resist the urge to only tell people about your business, products or services in your marketing. Most companies take this approach – and it doesn't work.

Chapter 21

9 Shortcuts for Writing Eyeball-Grabbing Headlines

L et's dig into the most important element in a lead-capturing marketing piece – the headline.

Copywriting legend Ted Nicholas, whose copy has sold more than $5.9 billion in products and services, suggests that 73% of all buying decisions are made at the headline.

Without exception, you need a headline in every marketing piece. Without one, you significantly limit your ability to attract attention in today's crowded marketplace.

So here are 9 shortcuts for writing headlines that grab eyeballs like glue:

1. Identify your buyer's big benefit. Just like the genie who appears from Aladdin's lamp, imagine telling your ideal prospect you can grant any wish related to your business. You might say:

"If I could give you any benefit or result using my service (or product), what would it be?"

Your prospect's response is what is often labeled a "hidden benefit." Nicholas used this strategy to sell more than 200,000 copies of his book, *How to Form Your Own Corporation Without a Lawyer for Under $75.* His headline read …

The Ultimate Tax Shelter
Here are a couple other examples:
I'll Sell Your Home in Fewer Than 45 Days or My Services are Free
Lose 14 Pounds a Month Doing Effortless Exercises

2. Target a specific prospect. You can temporarily disable your prospects' inner critic by calling attention to specific problems. After all, problems are "messages" your mind can relate to because you're actively thinking about them.

So use your headline to highlight problems you can help solve.

For golfers who are almost (but not quite) satisfied with their game – and can't figure out what they're doing wrong …

To online advertisers struggling to collect consistent leads – and can't figure out where to turn for honest advice …

Yes, this type of headline can get long. However, you can also use it as a lead-in to a more concise headline. Or, you can go shorter …

For the woman who feels older than her age …

For frustrated homeowners who owe much more than their homes are worth …

3. Pique curiosity. If your headline teases prospects with just enough facts that you leave them guessing, oftentimes they will buy your product or service simply to satisfy their curiosity.

The "Forgotten" Muscle That Can Increase Your Kicking Power by Up to 43%

FACT: 10% of a 2-Year-Old Pillow's Weight is From Dead Mites and Their Droppings

4. Explain "how to." The words "how to" promise a solution to a problem. The key is to follow up these words with a big benefit that addresses your prospects' greatest concerns. Of course, you then need to deliver quality information.

How to Legally Rob Banks

How to Take Great Photos Using Your Smart-phone and Free Apps

5. Create and/or enter the news. Keep in mind, your product or service doesn't need to be new to create news. It only needs to be new to your readers. You can also tie your product or service into current events.

A New Hope for Neck and Back Pain Sufferers

The Startling Fact About Facebook's Falling Stock That Can Protect Your Portfolio

(Be careful with "news" headlines. Many businesses use exaggerated claims and abuse terms such as "At last!" "Announcing ... ," "Finally!" and "Introducing.")

6. Ask a question. For best results, make sure the question connects to a topic your prospects want answered. Also, whenever possible, create questions your readers can't answer with a "yes" or "no" response. That way they must read further into your copy for the answer(s).

Is This Advice From Your CPA Causing You to Overpay on Your Taxes?

Are These Mistakes Keeping You From Re-building Your 401k and Shielding it From Catastrophic Losses (Again)?

7. Command your readers. Sometimes all your prospects need is a little direction. After all, few people make decisions without guidance.

Beat Colds, Cancer and Old Age ... with Sex!

Take This 30-Second Test Before You Renew Your Cell Phone Service

(Note: Health-related publications are a great place for swiping "command" headlines.)

8. Go against the grain. If there's a universal thought related to what you offer, go against that popular belief and you'll get noticed fast.

Why Washing Your Hands is a Dangerous (and Even Deadly) Habit

How Lack of Exercise Could Make You Healthier

9. Try testimonials. Sometimes a legitimate third-party endorsement is all you need to push readers deeper into your marketing piece. Just like other headline styles, target a specific problem your prospects want to eliminate.

"I Wish Someone Told Me These Sneaky Sales Tricks Before I Bought My Last Car!"

"My Eyesight Returned to Normal in a Single Day ..."

Chapter 22

6 Ways to Create New Content for Old Websites

H ow often do you challenge yourself with a goal and a promise to complete it by a certain date?

"I'll have it done by the end of the month," you say ... or *"By this time next year, things will be different."*

Then the deadline arrives, but your desire for change still remains because you didn't do enough to meet your goal.

Frustrating, isn't it?

Unfortunately, these unfinished tasks or desires steal your thoughts. That's why I want to address a marketing medium that – once complete – usually gets far less attention than it deserves ...

The business website.

The problem is fresh content. More specifically, most business websites don't have it. They're little more than outdated brochures with trivial information.

One big benefit of websites is the ability to instantly update content. You can change offers, build prospect lists, address questions or problems, post news in different formats, survey your audience, and much more in seconds – often at no cost.

(Of course, these actions assume you use a content management system such as WordPress. If you don't, make adding one to your website a priority.)

No other marketing medium offers more flexibility than your website.

So today I'm giving you several ideas for creating new content. Now, keep in mind, this isn't the typical content you're used to seeing on home, services, about us and contact pages. After all, I'm sure you already have those pages under control.

So here we go …

1. Create tutorials. Brainstorm challenges your prospects want to overcome as they relate to your product or service. Then write instructions or record videos of you talking/showing them through the processes. Spend a little time on YouTube and you'll notice the most popular videos describe how-to tasks. The same goes for Amazon.com and nonfiction books.

2. Compile lists. Numbered lists attract attention because they're quickly "scannable." Easy topics worth focusing on include myths, mistakes and misconceptions related to your offers. Remember, your prospects care more about solving their problems than buying your product or service. So make sure your content reflects this mindset.

3. Interview industry insiders and experts. Oprah built a business empire by sharing others' knowledge. Thanks to today's technology, you can do the same on a smaller scale and make the recordings (or written interviews/transcripts) available to a worldwide audience using your website.

4. Share statistics and studies. By sharing the latest industry trends and news – and providing your insight – you position yourself as a thought leader. Simply scan sites such as Quora.com and FactBrowser.com to find industry-related questions and studies to support your statements. Google Alerts can also help you stay on top of your industry's latest happenings.

5. Grant "behind-the-scenes" access. Who doesn't enjoy a peek into other people's lives? Facebook thrives off this single desire. Show how your business operates and the secrets to your success. This transparency builds trust.

6. Answer questions. While exact numbers aren't available, it's widely accepted that many online search queries are questions. Use this behavior to your advantage by creating individual pages for detailed responses to each of the most common questions you hear from prospects.

And one final suggestion ...

Use multiple media formats when creating your content. Sure, almost everyone reads content. But some in your audience may enjoy listening to audio or watching videos, too. Furthermore, using different media makes it easier to distribute your content in more places.

Chapter 23

What Determines Content Quality?

I often remind business owners and entrepreneurs to give away some of their best information when marketing.

By delivering value first, you prove to prospects you genuinely want to help them. You also begin laying a foundation of trust and credibility.

But what determines your content's value? How can you be certain what you share is viewed as quality information?

Well, the first step is to put yourself in your prospect's position. **If you were your prospect, would you be willing to pay for the information shared in your marketing materials?**

You should.

Next, take the focus off you. Make your marketing about your prospects. They want content that tells stories ... reveals secrets ... explains mistakes ... confirms or goes against their assumptions ... inspires action ... and solves their pressing problems.

So now go grab the last marketing piece you put in front of your prospects and review the content. If it doesn't meet the standards set by the above characteristics, you have work to do.

You want to make your marketing so valuable that prospects would cringe with anxiety if they had to throw it away.

Recently, I did some research online to find other criteria for quality content. I stumbled on a post from Google's webmaster blog that offered several conditions the search engine giant uses when determining content value on web pages (listed below).

What surprised me was how well the standards also applied to offline communication. I encourage you to use the following conditions when evaluating your next marketing piece:

- Would you trust the information in this article?

- Is this article written by an expert or enthusiast who knows the topic well, or is it more shallow in nature?

- Are the topics driven by genuine interests of readers of the site, or does the site generate content by attempting to guess what might rank well in search engines?

- Does the article provide original content, original reporting, original research, or original analysis?

- Does the page provide substantial value when compared to other pages in search results?

- Is the content mass-produced by or outsourced to a large number of creators, or spread across a large network of sites?

- Would you recognize this site as an authoritative source when mentioned by name?

- Does this article provide a comprehensive description of the topic?

- Does this article contain insightful analysis or interesting information that is beyond obvious?

- Is this the sort of page you'd want to bookmark, share with a friend, or recommend?

- Does this article have an excessive amount of ads that detract from the main content?

- Would you expect to see this article in a printed magazine, encyclopedia or book?

- Are the articles short, unsubstantial, or otherwise lacking in helpful specifics?

- Are the pages produced with great care and attention to detail?

- Would users complain when they see pages from this site?

You have the opportunity to create incredibly valuable content each time you communicate with prospects. Are you up to the task?

TRUST TRILOGY
PART II:

Trust requires consistent communication (because it creates familiarity).

Chapter 24

What's the Best Length for Marketing Materials?

Questions about content length are among the most frequent I hear from people creating marketing materials.

How many words should I write for my special report? How long should my videos be? Is there a proper length for blog posts or web pages?

The answer to all these questions is simple:

The best length is whatever you need to properly deliver your marketing message.

Mix up your length and formats. If length concerns keep you from creating content, you're worrying about the wrong issue.

Of course, different subjects merit different lengths. You can cover some topics in a short article, while others are better explained in a special report or book format. Still others might require a video screencast to show details that are difficult to communicate in writing.

Also, by creating length variety, you increase opportunities to reach more markets. If you can only teach how-to information by writing 50-100 pages at a time, you limit your audience.

Varied format and lengths also help ensure you don't get bored with the process. Monotony robs you of enthusiasm for just about any activity.

Some days you might feel a quick blog post is best. On days where your concentration (and time) is high, you might crank out an entire guide or record an hour-long podcast with minimal effort.

Regardless of what format you use most, content – of all lengths and styles – should be repurposed. Traditionally, when a business owner or entrepreneur creates a piece of content, it's largely forgotten after getting published. Therefore, those active in creating content for any length of time quickly develop a collection.

By combining already-published articles, blog posts, podcasts or videos, you can produce saleable products in a fraction of the time it typically takes to create one from scratch.

You can also present the information at seminars and workshops. Take this idea a step further by pulling select information to create a quick workbook for attendees. Offer it for free or a fee.

The bottom line is that content creates options when marketing your business. So instead of worrying about length, focus on pumping out as much helpful material as possible.

Chapter 25

Why So Much Marketing Creates Pricing Problems

What do you suppose is the easiest way to prevent prospects from using price to compare what you offer?

After all, cost is the most common factor when comparison shopping. Consumers search for deals. They crave value for their money.

Unfortunately, this causes problems for business owners, entrepreneurs and executives who market like their competitors.

You see, when your product or service – and its marketing – looks like everything else in your industry, you force prospects to use price as the deciding factor when buying.

As a result, the lowest price usually wins.

So unless you want the problems that come with being a low-cost provider, you must deliver a different marketing experience than your competition.

For example, ever notice how Beachbody promotes their fitness programs? While most fitness products promise a ripped physique and weight loss with minimal effort, programs like P90X and Insanity take the opposite approach.

Promotions use phrases such as "the world's most insanely tough workout" and "work harder than you've ever worked before." What's more, the programs cost far more than comparable fitness DVDs.

Yet Beachbody has reached $1.3 billion in sales and become a giant in the fitness industry.

When Ermias Asghedom (aka Nipsey Hussle) released a mixtape last October, instead of offering it for free online – as is the industry norm – he created marketing madness by pricing it at $100. All 1,000 CDs sold … in less than 24 hours.

Prior to the 2014 Super Bowl, the Old Homestead Steakhouse generated extensive media coverage by offering a $150,000 Super Bowl feast. The legendary eatery is no stranger to unique marketing. In 2005, it was the first New York eatery to put a burger priced over $40 on its menu.

Five years later, after Lady Gaga wore a meat dress to the 2010 MTV Video Music Awards, Old Homestead stole part of the publicity by creating its own costume. The 112 pounds of raw meat was then offered for sale at $100,000.

Of course, these are extreme examples – but the lesson remains the same.

Market differently or you force prospects to use price as the only factor when deciding whether to buy from you.

Chapter 26

How to Create Positive Positioning in Your Prospects' Minds

I f you ever analyze your mental conversations, you're likely aware of a tip that can help you write better marketing materials.

The fact is, people don't argue with themselves. (Can you imagine if they did?)

So when you take an idea they express in their minds and then mention it in your marketing, prospects are likely to agree with what you said.

That's why it's critical you match the language your prospects use to describe their situation.

For example, I'm a copywriter. But I don't use that term much outside marketing circles because it creates confusion for many entrepreneurs or executives. "Copywriter" just isn't a word many business professionals use.

But when I mention writing marketing materials that capture leads and often cut marketing costs at the same time, most people understand what I'm talking about.

Keep in mind, when you match mental thoughts, you tap into the repetition principle. And, as you know, repeated words or patterns are easier to remember. In addition, duplicating mental thoughts often causes people to accept what's repeated as being true.

And here's another thought to consider ...

Positive language creates positive mental conditioning. So if you want prospects to lean toward a "yes" response, put them in a positive state of mind.

A free item of value often starts the process. You can then pile on the positivity with your words.

Let's look at car insurance as an example. The typical pitch usually focuses on a negative situation, such as you're paying too much or don't have enough coverage.

Several years ago, GEICO modified this approach and began stressing a positive spin. Instead of reminding people that they might be getting ripped off, they began to talk about potential savings.

As a result, I bet you're now familiar with the company's catchphrase ...

Fifteen minutes could save you 15% or more on car insurance.

Notice the positive language? Do you think the statement would have the same effect if it said ...

Take 15 minutes to learn if you're spending too much on car insurance.

Who knows? Testing is the only way to tell for sure.

GEICO has gone from bankruptcy to become the nation's second-largest auto insurer. Of course, positive positioning isn't the only reason. (No doubt GEICO owner Warren Buffett plays a role in the company's success.)

But what they've done is separate themselves from the competition by pushing positivity. Other car insurance companies – such as Allstate and its Mayhem character – still focus on negative reasons for insurance coverage.

So what are some mental marketing strategies that you've found to be successful?

Chapter 27

An Overlooked List That Holds Hidden Profit Opportunities

I just stole something for you ...

As you know, my job gives me behind-the-scenes insight into how some of the world's greatest marketers handle "selling" problems in different ways. It's a great education that never quits.

And recently I saw a tremendous client reactivation idea ... tremendous because it works like magic and is rarely used in marketing efforts.

Credit goes to Ferd Nauheim. I recently bought his book, *Salesman's Complete Model Letter Handbook*, in which he shares many overlooked opportunities for communicating with clients and prospects. The book is especially helpful for those times when you want to contact someone but can't figure out what to say without sounding like a pushy salesman.

Anyway, I stole one of Nauheim's letters and reworked it for you. Don't worry, though, I'm certain he doesn't mind.

If fact, he states at the beginning of his book, *"In many cases, salesmen and sales managers will be able to use letters in this book with little or no change. But even where a complete change is required to fit a particular set of circumstances, the model letters point the way."*

In one section, Nauheim shares letters of appreciation to customers. The one I revised for you is designed to reactivate lost clients or those who haven't bought from you in a long time.

Use the following letter as a model. Simply copy and paste the text to your letterhead, make adjustments to fit your company, and then mail – with a stamp on a hand-addressed envelope – the letters to your lost clients.

Dear (enter client's first name),

It's been some time since I expressed my heartfelt thanks.

While looking at my calendar earlier this week, I thought about the thank-you notes I should send to two new clients. Then it suddenly occurred to me that, while saying thanks to folks who just bought from me may be good business, I never took the time to express my sincere appreciation to you for your loyalty over the years.

I'm concerned that something I did caused you to stay away for so long. If so, please contact me at (enter phone number) or (enter email address) so I can correct the problem.

Then again, maybe life's events just got in the way.

Whatever the case, I suppose I'm no more guilty than most people. We are so concerned with day-to-day business needs that we seldom take time out to show the great gratitude we feel for our most important business friends ... those who keep coming back and who thoughtfully send others to us.

I appreciate your continuing support.

Gratefully,
(enter your name/signature)

P.S. (Use this space to share an appealing offer and/or provide a strong reason to respond).

———

Sure, this letter isn't perfect. You could do things different. And you may even think the text won't work for you.

But that's not the point.

The fact to remember is you likely have a lost client list that holds hidden profit opportunities. Contact these people now.

Chapter 28

Why Marketing to Attract New Clients Can Be a Mistake

I t's crazy how so many marketing resources are directed toward finding new clients. What gets overlooked is the biggest barrier to a sale ...

Trust.

When trust levels increase, so does the likelihood of prospects opening their wallets. Without trust, sales become almost impossible.

You already established a trust level with past clients. So, logically, it takes less effort to get them to buy again.

On the other hand, attracting new clients requires more effort and resources because the trust isn't developed.

Remember, in many cases, past clients stopped doing business with you because they didn't have other opportunities. So what activities can you take now to encourage past or existing clients to do business with you again?

Not long ago, I received an email from Dick's Sporting Goods with the following subject line: *We've Missed You Tom – Come Back and Save 20%.*

Honestly, I can't remember the last time I bought anything from Dick's. But that doesn't mean I'm not willing to spend money with them.

Dick's just hasn't been on my shopping radar because the nearest location is 15 miles away. Several comparable options are much closer.

But, at the very least, I'll now keep Dick's in mind for upcoming purchases. Whereas before I didn't even consider the retailer.

My buddy, Charles Gaudet, founder of Predictable Profits, has a customer re-engagement strategy product. He's a big believer in communicating with past clients and offers these tips when writing reactivation letters:

- Thank clients for past business,

- Express concern for their absence,

- Ask if you did something wrong,

- Remind them why you previously did business together, and

- Make a limited-time offer to bring them back.

Whenever possible, I believe you should also personalize as many of your letters (or e-mails) as you can. So, for example, if you know a client's purchase history, reference it and relate that sale to your new offer.

Pretty easy, right?

I encourage you to designate – at least every month – specific activities for maintaining contact with clients. For example, send regular e-mails that educate clients about issues related to the product/service they bought from you. (You should already be creating this type of content for blog posts, videos and other inbound marketing activities.)

Also, don't overlook mailed newsletters. Few marketing pieces get greater readership than a printed newsletter that arrives the old-fashioned way – in mailboxes. Of course, in addition to helpful information, include an offer. You can even bundle a few products/services together to get larger sales with less effort.

Chapter 29

These Mistakes Cause You to Overspend on Marketing

L et's say you have one day to either run a full-page color or half-page black-and-white ad in your local newspaper (whose audience includes potential prospects).

Which would you choose?

Before making your choice, let me tell you about a client who faced an almost identical decision.

You see, he was running a full-page color ad once a week for several weeks a row. Disappointed with the response, he asked me for suggestions. So I proposed he change the format, eliminate color and slash the ad size in half.

In effect, I suggested he cut his costs and create a smaller ad that was less visually appealing (at least from a designer's perspective).

So what happened?

The first day the ad ran, his response was about 250% greater than all the previous weeks combined.

Not too bad, especially when you consider he dramatically decreased his costs by running a smaller ad without color. What's more, he now has a piece he can repeatedly run and – with relative certainty – know a response will follow.

The fact is, far too many entrepreneurs and executives believe bigger and colorful is better. Of course, that's not always the case.

Regardless of what medium you use, your best bet when marketing is to test small. Then, once you generate the response you want, invest those profits into larger materials and markets.

Any other approach only wastes money.

Let's say I handed you a post-it note with the winning numbers for tonight's lottery drawing. Would it matter if the numbers were written in black crayon or red pen?

Of course not!

Your marketing isn't any different. The value comes from the insight you share.

Sure, you want a clean look – but make delivering value your primary objective. Deliver strong stuff and response will follow.

And while we're on the topic of overspending when marketing ...

Pay close attention to who sees your message. A big audience doesn't always lead to a big response.

Sure, you can buy an email list with 250,000 names and spam your message to those people. But why blow your budget communicating with people who aren't familiar with (or even care about) what you offer?

I've run into many business owners who were lured into buying an audience that didn't include their prospects. Sure, you can run a "cheap" announcement in your church bulletin and reach many people. But what's the point if they aren't your prospects?

Let me give you another example ...

While recently working on a mailing with a motorcycle accident attorney, we noticed several contacts provided by the list broker included people who owned off-road bikes. My client only serves motorcyclists who ride road bikes.

So we cut those names from his list and, as a result, instantly lowered his mailing costs. After all, it was pointless for us to communicate with those people.

Take a close look today at where you might be overspending on your marketing. Of course, if you need help uncovering savings, while generating a better response, the tips in this book are a great place to start.

Chapter 30

This Persuasion Tool Fixes Buying Resistance

K now the feeling you get when someone you just met is about to hit you with a sales pitch?

Maybe you noticed an awkward attempt to build rapport or thought the communication sounded too rehearsed to be believable – and now you're certain the situation is about to get more uncomfortable.

This experience is common, isn't it?

Well, the reality is people interested in certain products or services avoid situations where salespeople are involved. That's why it's critical for you to elevate your status.

Here's one way to do it:

Mimic the behavior of influential leaders in your industry.

One fact you'll notice is industry thought leaders – those people who have the most influence and success – consistently publish content. This action isn't by accident. Written words hold incredible power.

Consistently published content creates authority status. It is also an effective persuasion tool that helps break your prospects' buying resistance.

Of course, content in a book format has the greatest impact, especially if you want to be seen as an industry expert. But these days you have many other options.

You can use e-mail, a blog or a newsletter. You can record a recurring podcast. You can pick up a camera and start shooting videos. You can even respond to industry-specific questions people post online.

In addition to consistency, the key is making your content valuable. After all, great content gets shared in today's socially connected world.

Remember, content is the currency that drives marketing. Instead of money, you exchange content for your prospects' attention.

When you don't have content (or content that's not consistently updated), your prospects direct attention elsewhere.

Also keep in mind, the more you create content that helps your prospects solve their problems, the more they'll reward you with engagement and sales.

Chapter 31

How to Create Content When You Have Nothing New to Say

Let's solve a problem that sounds a little something like this …
"I don't have anything new to say" or *"I don't know anything that my competitors don't already know."*

Too often business owners and entrepreneurs fall back on these justifications when explaining why they don't create helpful content for prospects. They believe the information they share must be an original concept.

But this is not the case.

Keep in mind, you have a distinctive style when you present material. Your unique voice resonates with certain people, while others prefer an alternative source.

In fact, even when you share identical concepts as your competitors, no two people take away the same ideas.

For instance, look at late-night television. Jimmy Fallon and Jimmy Kimmel both interview celebrity friends and offer humorous takes on pop culture. Both target the 18-49 demographic and have a knack for viral videos. And both use the Internet and social media to expand their audiences.

But, if you watch late-night television, you likely have a favorite. You prefer one over the other, right?

The fact is, the more you share helpful information, the more you attract the prospects you want. Prospects seek out people they like and trust. And, by helping them, you prove you care about their needs – not just the money you hope they bring you.

Your content offers a glimpse into your personality and perspective. When prospects like what you share, they naturally crave more.

This desire especially works to your advantage when you have big-brand competitors. Thanks to legal fears, many larger companies must deliver sterile, heavily scripted marketing messages that offer little feeling.

You don't have this restriction.

What's more, with common concepts, you have the freedom to add your own experiences. Or, to really attract attention, go against familiar claims.

For instance, I used this strategy a few years ago with an article titled *Why a Website is a Worthless Investment*. I received several responses from confused readers. With so many marketing experts touting the need for a website, why did I recommend something different?

Well, it wasn't that I believed you shouldn't have a website. Instead, I used the contrarian approach to first attract attention. Then, I used the article to show how simply having a website is not enough to generate revenue from an online audience.

(In case you're wondering, here are the four website "musts" I mentioned in the article:

- Keep your content fresh and formatted for the search engines,

- Target appropriate keywords and phrases,

- Develop a consistent way to convert your visitors to buyers, and

- Provide information your prospects desire.)

Chapter 32

These Places Have 'Starving' Crowds of Buyers

The story is legendary in marketing circles …

Gary Halbert, who many consider one of the greatest copywriters ever, often talked about one of his favorite questions to ask while presenting classes on copywriting and selling by mail.

"If you and I both owned a hamburger stand and we were in a contest to see who would sell the most hamburgers, what advantages would you most like to have on your side?" he'd ask.

The answers often varied. Some people wanted superior meat. Others mentioned location. And still others expressed a desire for the lowest prices.

After hearing all the answers, Halbert would make his request:

"Okay, I'll give you every single advantage you asked for. I, myself, only want one advantage and, if you will give it to me, I will whip the pants off of all of you when it comes to selling burgers!"

Of course, everyone was anxious to hear what advantage is so beneficial. You're probably wondering the same thing, right?

"The only advantage I want," he'd reply, *"is a starving crowd!"*

You see, Halbert encouraged business owners and entrepreneurs to watch for groups of people who demonstrated that they are starving (or at least hungry) for a particular product or service.

Thanks to the Internet, these types of prospects are accessible, especially when they search for content related to a product or service. You just have to make sure your content is available for them to consume.

Think about it ...

When someone goes to a website such as Amazon.com, they search for content, right? In fact, they're willing to pay for it.

So if you don't have content on Amazon.com, you're missing opportunities to get your message in front of a worldwide audience – a group of buyers that grows bigger every day.

Now, you don't have to write a book (although you should – or least a special report). You can quickly get on Amazon.com with just an MP3 recording.

According to a new Forrester report, Amazon.com now outpaces Google and other search engines as the place where shoppers begin online searches.

To upload your content to Amazon.com for free, use either CreateSpace (for books and audio downloads) or kdp.amazon.com (to self-publish your content in the Kindle Store).

YouTube is another place where crowds flock. Check out these statistics:

- More than 88 million people watch an online video on a given day.

- Online video is currently 40% of consumer Internet traffic.

- 75% of C-suite executives watch work-related videos weekly.

Create a YouTube account and you can immediately upload your videos ... for free. Again, YouTube is a place where people search for content.

Why shouldn't you be the person providing it?

Also, if you record podcasts, put them on iTunes. The iTunes Store has more than 150,000 free podcasts available and recently surpassed

1 billion subscribers. Once someone subscribes to your podcast, iTunes automatically downloads new episodes to that person's iTunes library.

That means your marketing message gets uploaded on your subscribers' iPods (and similar devices) whenever you post something new. Not to mention, your material is always accessible to searchers (and new potential subscribers) in the iTunes library.

And let's not forget about other websites and blogs within your industry. Find ones that have regular readers and then ask the site/blog's owner if you can write a guest post. You can also make this same request to offline publications. Small, local newspapers and newsletters especially need new content.

Whatever option you choose, don't forget to drive your audience back to a place where you can collect contact information. That way you can follow up and continue delivering educational material that further develops the relationship with your new audience.

Chapter 33

Simple Ways to Make Your Media Message More Appealing

While going through a recent issue of Dan Kennedy's *No B.S. Marketing Letter*, I read a piece by Steve Harrison, who has helped more than 12,000 authors and entrepreneurs land radio/TV, print and online publicity.

He shared several tips for securing publicity and making the media love you.

Harrison's suggestions started with a basic tip – "Keep it short." We know time is tight for the media because they have strict deadlines. So a concise inquiry is almost always necessary.

Next, he encouraged delivering "specific and vivid" information. The key idea here is to take an otherwise boring statistic, trend, event, etc. and make it memorable. **Too often, sources share insight that's so basic it seems repetitious.**

After reading this tip, I couldn't help but think of how the media gravitates to certain sports stars when they need memorable quotes. For example, one time when former NBA basketball player Charles Barkley was asked to recall his thoughts about retiring before his final season, he told a reporter:

"I remember sitting down with the Rockets and saying, 'Yeah. I'm going to retire.' They said, 'Well, we'll give you $9 million.' And I said, 'You got a pen on you?'"

From a media perspective, a humorous quote like this one creates a more entertaining article, video highlight or feature story.

The third tip Harrison shares is "express a solid opinion." Too often, people say what they believe others want to hear. **Don't be afraid to state your beliefs, even if your comments might attract critics.**

Here's one of my favorite quotes to use in press releases:

"Unfortunately, there's a deadly misconception that budget determines the effectiveness of a marketing campaign. This leads many budget-strapped business owners to do nothing, which is like waving the white flag and surrendering your company's future to luck."

The concept goes against beliefs shared by many business owners and entrepreneurs. As such, it piques curiosity and lures the media deeper into the release, where tips about marketing without a budget await.

In his article, Harrison mentioned Robert Thompson, a Syracuse University professor who sometimes fields up to 80 media calls in a day. Thompson suggests repeating words to make your quotes memorable.

For instance, about Paris Hilton, Thompson said, *"She's the non-story that keeps on being a non-story."*

Another suggestion is to compare something foreign with something familiar. Richard Branson is famous for saying, *"Business opportunities are like buses – there's always another one coming."*

Here's the same type of quote, only this one explains how social media applies to politics:

"Politics is the good-looking older guy who gets what's going on. Social media is the young media-savvy woman with a type-A personality. Things like Twitter and Facebook make politics look cool."

Notice how both quotes help make an unfamiliar idea clearer by relating it to a common item.

The final tip involves metaphors. **By "speaking" in metaphors, you can often create imagery – resulting in more memorable messages.** You create metaphors when you unite two unlike items that have something important in common.

The most effective metaphors stick in people's minds because they're unusual.

A few years ago, the media often referred to Sarah Palin as *"the rock star of the Republican party."* Then she became *"a lightning rod for criticism."*

If describing ways for kids to stay warm when playing outside, you might say, *"A heavy coat is a suit of armor."* Or you might warn that, *"The winter winds are a violent, stinging slap in the face."*

Now, from this day forward, each time you communicate with a member of the media, share at least one statement that's so unforgettable no story would be complete without including your message.

Chapter 34

What's the Best Bait for Catching Leads?

A couple years ago I took my kids fishing to several ponds not far from our home.

The surroundings were perfect. Not only were few people around, but the shore was shaded (much needed in the Phoenix heat) and we could see fish swimming when we first walked to the edge.

I knew catching dinner was a sure thing. So I slid a couple worms on hooks and encouraged the kids to start casting.

Not a minute later, I heard a line getting reeled in. Mary was bringing in her bait – she wanted to cast again.

Alex soon followed Mary's lead … and the chorus of continuous casting began.

Of course, this activity made catching fish nearly impossible. So I shared fatherly fishing wisdom with my two wannabe anglers …

"You can't catch fish without bait in the water," I stressed.

The statement became the day's motto. Even though I repeated it often, the kids kept casting as we moved from pond to pond.

As you can probably guess, no fish found our hooks that day.

Too often I see business owners and entrepreneurs make a similar mistake when marketing. They fish for leads, but they lack the right bait to attract prospects.

Worse yet, many don't offer any bait at all!

You might see a phone number or website, but the marketing piece doesn't include a reason to take action … there's no promised value.

Your prospects are under a continuous assault from marketing messages. You must offer exceptional value if you expect your lead-generating offer to attract attention.

Especially for service-based businesses, I urge you to stay away from using "free consultation" in your marketing. Sure, you can provide consultations, but stop using the term in your promotional pieces.

Think about why …

How many businesses offer consultations as a way to lure prospects? When you only use a "free consultation" to generate leads, you instantly label yourself as equal to others in your industry.

Furthermore, you make it too easy for prospects to compare your consultation (without taking you up on your offer) with any others they already experienced – even if the businesses weren't related to yours.

As a result, it becomes too easy to ignore your offer.

If you offer a consultation in your marketing, give it a unique name. For example, if you're a tax attorney, you might offer a "Tax Lien Settlement Session." Then (and this step is critical) describe what your prospects can expect by meeting with you.

Many people hesitate to inquire about consultations, fearing they'll only get an aggressive pitch. Calm this fear in your marketing and you'll get more leads.

Chapter 35

Must-Have Tools for Marketing Success

A couple summers ago, I stared in disbelief from the porch at my mom and stepdad's house in Ludington, Michigan, as a neighbor cut the bushes around his home.

No doubt, the hedges hadn't met a trimmer in many months. They had grown to at least 7 feet high.

I gawked as the guy struggled to hack branches the size of small fence posts. His chosen tool was a little electric trimmer that he swung over his head to reach the highest limbs.

My stepdad, who first the noticed the neighbor's struggles, walked over and offered his ladder and other tools – but his proposition was declined.

The bushes ended up a mangled mess. What's more, a job that could have been completed in 30 minutes lasted two days.

The situation is a classic example of not choosing the right tools for the job. And many business owners and entrepreneurs make this same mistake when marketing. They overlook the proper tools for success.

Here are 3 necessities:

1. **An educational special report.** A "how-to" guide packed with useful information is essential to positioning you as an authority and trustworthy source (especially among skeptical prospects). It also helps you attract leads, instead of always having to chase them down.

   Not only can you use your special report on websites, but it's also ideal as a no-risk offer in print advertisements, radio spots, postcards, client reactivation letters, social media and many other campaigns.

2. **A list.** Share your special report in an exchange for a piece of contact information and you now own an ever-growing prospect list. But having this luxury doesn't mean you can ignore past clients. After all, these people already spent money with you – and, in many cases, will do so again when given the opportunity.

   Whether you communicate with your list(s) through email, snail mail, phone or other means, make sure you add value every time. Don't market what you want to say. Instead, give people what they need to succeed.

3. **An occasional "let-it-go" approach**. Entrepreneurs are guilty of trying to do it all. Many (including me) find it tough to step away from activities that solve a problem within their company. So they squander time and resources coming up with a passable solution, instead of letting someone with a more suitable skill set resolve the situation.

   I like how Dan Sullivan, considered the world's foremost expert on entrepreneurship in action, explained this concept during a recent 10x Talk. He said, "Everybody has something they're great at. The more they can free themselves up to just concentrate on that thing, the richer their life becomes."

Chapter 36

Are These Really the Most Persuasive Words in the English Language?

O ne of the most popular posts on the copywriting blog Copyblogger is titled *The 5 Most Persuasive Words in the English Language.* The piece received considerable attention in marketing circles – and with good reason. There isn't a business owner or entrepreneur (me included) who isn't looking for shortcuts on ways to persuade prospects, especially through writing.

Admittedly, I first read the title with skepticism. I thought the suggestions might be hype words that scream "big sale" or "discount." But, after reading the post, I agree the words can work well in situations where you need attention and action.

So, before going any further, here are "the most persuasive words in English":

• You

• Free

• Because

- Instantly

- New

The key with each word is understanding why it's effective. Just placing one anywhere in a marketing piece doesn't guarantee responses anymore than having a fishing pole on Alaska's Kenai River guarantees catching salmon.

"You" is a word I obviously love. So much so that I wrote a book – *The "You" Effect: How to Transform Ego-Based Marketing Into Captivating Messages That Create Customers* – focused on how to use it in your marketing copy.

During a time when many companies prefer self-promotional approaches to marketing, "you" stands out like a black bear in a sheep herd because the word tells prospects your message is for them.

If I was a betting man, "free" would be my pick as the most-used word in marketing history. A free option almost always gets consideration when creating offers.

Nowadays, though, skepticism is high. So even giveaways must have strong appeal to incite action.

Keep in mind, "free" may attract people, but that doesn't mean they're buyers. Be careful of people who latch on only looking for a free ride to advice.

As for "because," its effectiveness is often supported by a study mentioned by Robert Cialdini in his book *Influence: The Psychology of Persuasion.* Harvard social psychologist Ellen Langer went into a library and attempted to cut in front of several people lined up to use the copier. She tested different requests to see which one would result in the highest compliance rate.

"Excuse me, I have five pages. May I use the Xerox machine because I have to make some copies?" resulted in 93% of the people giving up their space in line.

Surprisingly, she experienced this high success rate even though she didn't provide a motive or extra information that would warrant anyone taking action. All she did was add the word "because" and restate the obvious.

The word "instantly" targets society's desire for immediate gratification. We are a culture that craves quick outcomes with minimal effort.

Fortunately, today's technology allows you to deliver instant information when marketing –whether through autoresponders, software, apps, text message or online downloads.

And, finally, "new" ...

Is there a company that better demonstrates the benefits of "new" more than Apple? When the company updates existing products, demand is staggering.

But the desire for the latest items isn't limited to technology.

When old brands want to look new again (or even relevant), they frequently turn to younger spokespeople. For example, Procter & Gamble's Oil of Olay, a 50-year-old brand, became "new" to many youthful women when it hired 29-year-old country singer Carrie Underwood as its brand ambassador.

In fact, Procter & Gamble uses this strategy often, applying it to other familiar brands such as Old Spice (with Terry Crews), Pantene (with Zooey Deschanel) and Gillette (with Andre 3000).

So what do you think? Do you use these five words when marketing? Which one do you find most effective?

Chapter 37

How to Get Big Engagement From Small Email Lists

I recently had a ridiculous service experience while visiting the deli at a nearby grocery store.

My daughter's birthday was two days away and she wanted a large party sub for the family get-together.

As I approached the counter, I noticed only one customer nearby. Several employees were behind the glass display that showcased all sorts of meats, cheeses and salads. So I figured I'd get help within seconds.

But the seconds soon turned to minutes.

I couldn't figure out why I was essentially invisible to the deli staff. At 6'5", 235 pounds, I don't blend in well with most surroundings.

Then I noticed one of those "please take a number" dispensers. So I pulled off the numbered paper.

And wouldn't you know it ... I was almost instantly greeted by a response. *"How can I help you?"* asked a lady behind the counter.

I couldn't help but think – as cliché as it sounds – I was literally "just a number" to the deli staff. My needs really didn't matter and I was certain my order wouldn't get any special attention.

Unfortunately, as much as business owners and entrepreneurs hate to admit it, prospect and client email lists are often viewed in a similar manner. Size (in numbers) is seen as the primary factor when determining success. And, as a result, small lists get little attention.

What you might not realize is you have an advantage when your audience is small. You can give those people attention that would otherwise be difficult with a larger crowd.

For example, instead of sending a mass mailing each time you communicate to your list, why not try an individual e-mail for each person? This works especially well for subscribers who just signed up for your opt-in offer.

Personal attention is an easy way to start the engagement process. You might start by asking about specific problems you can help solve.

Also, remind new subscribers that you respond to inquiries yourself. Simply telling them you're open to communication will lead to more engagement.

If you have a blog (and you should), use your question responses to create posts. Imagine the impact you'd make with a prospect if she saw an entire article on your website dedicated to answering her question.

Understand, as well, that email isn't your only option for engagement. A small audience makes face-to-face conversations easier, too. Today's technology allows for easy communication with an audience via video – and you don't need any special equipment.

So schedule an online chat. You can "Hangout" on Google with as many as nine other people at a time.

Spreecast is another online option for communicating with multiple people at the same time via video. And, of course, Skype is available for one-on-one chats.

Keep in mind, just as with content, attention is a form of currency when marketing.

When people share their interest with you, give them an experience beyond their expectations and you'll be rewarded with loyalty.

Chapter 38

An Overlooked Marketing Strategy for Raising Your Prices

What makes someone eagerly buy a product or service that's priced at least two times more than comparable options?

You might be surprised to know that, in certain cases, the decision comes down to something as simple as a piece of paper.

Let me explain …

My wife, Michelle, and I recently stopped at Bed, Bath & Beyond for new bed pillows. She replaced the last set without me. So I went into the store not really knowing what to expect.

I groaned the instant we set foot in the pillow section. The price range was ridiculous – and all the items looked the same!

Prices for the puffy white rectangles started at $19.99 and went as high as $159.99.

Confused, I immediately grabbed a middle-of-the-road option. After all, my only buying criterion was avoiding the cheapest, low-quality choices.

Michelle, on the other hand, zeroed in on a high-end model that was at least twice as much as my pillow. When I asked about her preference, Michelle explained she wasn't sleeping well and believed the pillow she picked would solve the problem.

I rested my head on her pillow. It felt the same as mine and, of course, looked identical.

The only difference?

The label showed Michelle's pillow was recommended by sleep expert and *New York Times* best-selling author Dr. James B. Maas. What's more, the packaging included Dr. Maas' sleep tips booklet, which is an excerpt from his book *Sleep for Success! Everything You Must Know About Sleep But Are Too Tired To Ask.*

Although the booklet was just a few saddle-stitched pieces of paper, the information inside represented tremendous value to Michelle. After all, the topic matched the thoughts in her mind (i.e., I need a pillow that helps me sleep better.).

Think about this for a minute …

Knowledge shared on little pieces of paper caused my wife to spend twice the medium price for a commoditized product. And you know she's not the only one buying those pillows.

I often talk about how you writing a marketing piece from scratch is like an artist with a blank canvas. Your written words serve as the "paint" that determines what prospects are willing to pay for your product or service.

The closer you match their problems, the higher the price they'll pay.

Search for Dr. Maas' pillows on the Bed, Bath & Beyond website and you'll see another smart marketing move. All seven pillows (only one was available in the store) target a specific type of sleeper or problem.

For example, he offers options for people who sleep on their side, stomach and back, as well as those who feel stressed or enjoy reading in bed.

Dr. Maas doesn't offer pillows like everyone else. He delivers solutions to specific problems and uses his marketing to prove it. As a result, he can charge higher prices.

So how well do you target your prospects' problems in your marketing? Do you deliver solutions – or only pitch what you offer and hope people buy?

Chapter 39

Why Context Can Kill Your Marketing

I f you want your marketing to trigger strong appeal, here's a concept you can't overlook:

Prospects decide whether your marketing message is worthy of attention by assessing quality <u>and</u> context.

Let me give you an example that explains what I mean ...

Imagine you sit down on your couch tonight, turn on your TV and see Paul McCartney playing his guitar on stage at New York City's Madison Square Garden.

Even if you didn't recognize the former Beatle or were unfamiliar with his music, would you view him as someone with a high level of musical talent?

You probably would. After all, he's on TV and performing at a venue billed as "The World's Most Famous Arena."

Right?

Okay, now let's imagine you saw him playing the same guitar. However, this time he was singing alone on a street corner, dressed in casual clothes and seeking donations.

How would you view his talent? Would you still consider him a world-class performer?

A similar scenario played out in 1984. McCartney was filming a movie called *Give My Regards to Broad Street*. During production, producers put him in front of a London railway station and asked him to perform his song *Yesterday*, one of the most covered songs in recorded music history.

Much to McCartney's surprise, not one person recognized him. Passing people viewed the singer as just another street performer. So they saw little reason to pay much attention.

Crazy, isn't it?

An entertainer described by Guinness World Records as the "most successful composer and recording artist of all time" was instantly transformed into an ordinary musician because of a change in environment.

You likely experience this phenomenon, too. For example, how often do give greater trust to published material? After someone writes a book or gets published in a high-profile publication, credibility follows.

You could post identical information on a pile of napkins (or even a flier, email or website) and it wouldn't carry a fraction of the credibility offered by a published piece.

How and where you use your marketing materials determines the importance prospects place on them.

So write for industry publications … establish yourself as an author … speak in front of audiences … create and lead industry groups … form your own networks … distribute information worth sharing … interview your field's most famous faces … and, above all, use your marketing to show compassion and a desire for helping people.

Chapter 40

The Routine Shared by Today's Most Successful Marketers

E very once in a while, I get pushback from a potential client after presenting a project fee.

The response usually sounds something like: *"That's a little more than I was expecting to pay"* or *"I was hoping I wouldn't have to spend more than _____."*

After doing a little digging, I find the pushback is almost always the result of a single problem ...

The prospect views marketing as an expense, rather than an asset.

This mistake prevents companies from marketing on a consistent basis. Since marketing is only seen as a means to spend money, the expense is avoided until gathering leads becomes a necessity. Then marketing turns into a single event where time becomes the enemy and prospects' needs get ignored.

You might try a tradeshow booth ... run an ad in a newspaper ... buy and blast a list with an offer ... record your first video ... get in touch with the last SEO "expert" who promised a first-page ranking ... or look for some other shortcut.

This mentality is no different from the husband who shops for flowers the day after a forgotten wedding anniversary. Sure, the concept is correct – but it's often too late!

Companies that consistently generate leads treat marketing as a routine. Distributing a message that attracts prospects and creates clients is done just as much when business booms as when it slows.

Remember, effective marketing results in assets you can use over and over again.

In my business, for example, I have published books, special reports, hundreds of blog posts, articles in print publications, educational videos, audio recordings/podcasts and multiple websites that generate leads. I've been adding to these assets since October 2001, and they'll continue to produce as long as I make them available.

The likelihood of leads jumps each time I create content. So I strive to put out new material _at least_ once a week.

Listen, you have an incredible opportunity right now. It's never been easier to create and distribute marketing content – both online and offline.

You only have to be willing to make sharing your knowledge part of your routine.

Heck, you can begin with your website. Imagine what adding one piece of quality content to your website a week would do for your online presence.

Search engines love fresh content. So, at the very least, you'll increase your traffic.

And here's something else to keep in mind …

What if you take one of those new pieces from your website and use it other places?

Maybe you share it offline as part of a letter to re-connect with former clients … use it to maintain communication with a prospect email list …. make a few adjustments and send it to the media as a press release … add it to a monthly newsletter … insert it as a chapter for a future book … post it to your social media feeds … expand the subject to create a special report … apply it to a webinar or teleseminar …

Your options are almost limitless – and we're only talking about one piece of content!

Of course, creating content as part of a marketing routine isn't easy. Then again, when was the last time you took on a worthwhile task that was?

Chapter 41

An SEO 'Shortcut' You Can Use to Get Leads

Recently, I had a phone call with a member of a client's search engine optimization team. The first five minutes were painful and, unfortunately, the anguish only intensified the longer we talked.

You see, my client's website dropped in the search engines. So his SEO guy and I were discussing what caused the crash.

The culprit was a problem you've likely heard of ...

Duplicate content.

In an effort to keep content fresh, chunks of industry-related articles were pulled from other sites and then added to my client's blog. Post after post used content that appeared – in many instances – on multiple websites.

I see this happen a lot.

Instead of writing their own material, business owners and entrepreneurs try to shortcut the SEO process by using content from other places. In some cases, entire pages get posted word-for-word.

Although not as common nowadays, I also see websites with feeds that automatically add identical content from outside sources.

If you use one of these SEO shortcuts, I urge you to stop today.

Now, let me be clear ...

I'm a direct-response copywriter – not an SEO expert. But I regularly see how trying to trick the search engines into higher rankings causes trouble. I also repeatedly see how creating helpful, properly written content can attract the right traffic – and get those people to take action.

So here's the SEO "shortcut" I suggest:

Create content that truly helps people.

This concept isn't new. You won't see it talked about as an "insider secret." And, let's be honest, useful website content takes longer to create.

Of course, these are the reasons why serving website visitors with value isn't for everyone.

Keep in mind, people now consume more content than ever before. They're also more selective about what receives attention.

Look at your own situation …

Many e-mails go unread. Much of your mail ends up in the trash. Most content competing for your attention (especially online) gets ignored because it doesn't deliver what you need.

Simply put, information only becomes a priority when it's seen as useful.

Chapter 42

Why Marketing Can Cause Brain 'Blindness'

How many times have you spent minutes scanning a supermarket shelf in search of a specific item?

Maybe you couldn't find Fruity Pebbles in the cereal aisle ... or saffron among the spices ... or, as was the case with me on a recent Sunday, corn starch among a slew of baking supplies.

When this happens, you feel blind ... and, to a certain extent, you are.

A.K. Pradeep describes this condition in his book, *The Buying Brain: Secrets for Selling to the Subconscious Mind*, as "repetition blindness." The occurrence happens when the brain sees too many of the same objects. And, since it can't determine variations, everything gets blended together.

For example, let's go back to the cereal aisle at your local grocery store. The boxes have similar colors, shapes, phrases and graphics, right?

Well, it's this lack of differences that makes finding a specific brand a slow process.

Here's Pradeep's explanation on how your brain works in this situation:

*"**We're biologically programmed to seek differences.** To seek out things that enable us to make sense out of the environment we find ourselves in and to navigate our world safely and productively. When the brain is presented with a series of repetitive images – even if there are some differences among them – repetition blindness sets in. The brain no longer "sees" each individual image as it would if that image stood alone, or with only a small number of similar/identical images."*

Of course, the grocery store isn't the only place where repetition blindness occurs. It happens in all types of comparison situations.

And, obviously, marketing is not an exception.

As a consumer, you know this. Every day you subconsciously tune out most marketing messages, while giving your attention to a select few.

The messages you reward with interest have distinctive differences or target a desire you're actively thinking about, correct?

Too many business owners and entrepreneurs ignore this fact when creating their marketing. They look to competitors for ideas and then try to match whatever they see.

When you take this approach, you create more repetitive images in your prospects' minds. You disregard the brain's biologically programmed preference for differences. And, as a result, your message drowns in a sea of sameness.

Chapter 43

The Quickest Way to Go Broke When Marketing

Y ou and I both know your marketing should bring you business. But that's not to say it happens.

The truth is most marketing fails because attention is focused on the wrong subjects. Messages get ignored because they don't deliver content prospects want.

You don't have to look far to see brands blasting out one-way, ego-based messages about their companies or products/services. *"Look at us … look at us … we're great and we want to help you,"* screams their marketing.

Of course, this crappy content kills marketing efforts—but there's something else that drains marketing budgets like a flushed toilet bowl …

Targeting the wrong audience.

Your best bet when marketing is to communicate with people who already expressed interest in what you offer. (On a side note, this is why you should never stop delivering information that adds people to your prospect list.)

When you enter the convincing game and try to convert people's beliefs about why they need your product or service, you invite marketing disasters.

Let's look at politics (a topic I often avoid) as an example. It amazes me how many people volunteer their political views in public with the hopes of seeking support.

When someone pushes their political opinions on you, especially when those beliefs differ from yours, how do you feel?

It's frustrating, right? In some instances, you probably want to fire back with your opinions.

These feelings are due to the *consistency principle*. **Once we make up our minds about an issue, we naturally prefer to stay consistent about that thought.**

In fact, when that belief gets attacked, the instinctive reaction is to take a stubborn stand and fight stronger for your thoughts.

The greater the push, the stronger the belief becomes.

So when you try to convince people why they need what you offer, you fight a no-win battle.

Now do you understand why trying to convince people in your marketing is so expensive?

Instead of spending time (and your marketing budget) on people who you think need what you offer, direct your efforts toward those who demonstrate desire for the solution provided by your product or service.

TRUST TRILOGY
PART III:

Your marketing must develop relationships before it can drive profits.

Chapter 44

Don't Rob Your Prospects of Their Scarcest Resource

E ver notice how many people want to steal your scarcest resource? They crave a piece of your time, often for their own benefit. But this theft isn't only limited to people...

Each day hundreds of marketing messages attempt to rob you of your time, too.

So how do you decide where to direct your attention?

Well, fortunately, this decision mostly happens on an unconscious level. If you were consciously aware of every marketing message competing for your interest, you couldn't function.

Good thing you have instinct, that gut feeling that tells you (in a split second) when something isn't worth your time. When marketing to prospects, you must overcome this intuition if you have any chance at getting your message seen or heard.

Just like you, your prospects recognize promotional fluff.

Your gut knows advertisements; your gut knows when someone is selling; your gut knows when something serves someone else's interests.

Am I right?

Remember, the most effective marketing often doesn't look like marketing.

So, with this concept in mind, let me give you a challenge ...

When you write your next marketing piece, honor your prospects' time by presenting information as if they were already your clients/ customers.

Ignore your desires. Forget about selling. Disregard your competitors. Snub the internal voice that screams, "You're giving away too much!"

Take this exercise seriously and I guarantee your marketing grabs more eyeballs and gains greater interest.

Chapter 45

How You Can Create Effective Copy Without Writing a Single Word

Just about everyone who lacks a desired skill wants the secret shortcut to success – and copywriting is no different.

People want the 'magic' words that trigger action ... proven formulas for persuasion ... or how to write a single e-mail that sets off a surge in sales.

Well, the reality is that learning to write effective copy takes time and lots of writing. You see, copywriting is similar to a skill such as ice skating. You just can't learn how to glide across the ice by reading a book, watching videos or listening to instructions. You have to actually tie on some skates and step out on the ice.

Sure, you can pick up a copywriting trick or two by reading or even going through a training. But there's no replacement for putting pen to paper or clicking the keys on your keyboard.

That being said ...

I'll let you in on the simple skill that's been the foundation for my most effective copy. The good news is you already own this talent. But it's likely you haven't grasped how to apply it to your copywriting.

In fact, I overlooked it for a long time, too.

The skill I'm talking about is best described in the following ad headline written by legendary copywriter Eugene Schwartz:

I Write With My Ears

That's right, the simple skill is listening.

Check out these first four paragraphs from Schwartz's ad. They'll likely change how you write your next marketing piece.

Copywriting is the simplest of all possible jobs. It consists solely of turning items into ads, of making the physical verbal, of constructing an emotional holograph of the product so convincing that people will part with their good money to share it.

To produce copy, therefore, is not really to write it into being, but to listen it into being. In other words, to be a semi-passive conduit between the producer of the item, and its needer. Between the man who makes it do what it does, and the other man – somewhere out there – who needs what it does.

The first step, therefore – the essential step – in turning an item into an ad, is turning yourself into a listener.

You listen two ways: first with your ears, and then with your eyes. You hear everything you can about the product, and then you read everything you can about the product.

Now, let's be honest ...

Listening is tough. Talking is much easier, as is writing what you think prospects should know about your product or service.

Right?

But that's also why most copy doesn't convert.

I feel fortunate that I'm naturally introverted. Especially in unfamiliar situations, I'd rather sit silently and let others grab the spotlight.

Once I figured out I could use this characteristic to my advantage, I started recording all my client conversations. Radio Shack engineering enabled me to wire an old-school tape recorder to my desk phone – and I began gathering copy gold.

I recorded and listened to calls so often that the ribbons on my three tapes warped and the sounds became unintelligible. Fortunately, I've since been saved by a VoicePath™ device that links to recording software on my computer.

The following questions are among my favorites to ask when preparing copy:

- What is the competition for your service? Who are the major competitors? What are their failings? Is there a gap in the marketplace? If so, how does your service fill that gap? What do you offer that's exclusive?

- What are your prospects' biggest concerns, emotions and needs? What information or help does he/she need to deal with them?

- What is the story that led to the creation of your product/service?

- What are the most common questions your prospects have that prevent them from buying your product/service?

- What proof do you have that your product works?

- What problems were you trying to solve when you created your product/service?

These questions result in responses that go beyond the basic features you see promoted on most marketing materials. They also tie into the reasons your prospects respond to marketing.

I encourage you to ask yourself these questions before you write your next marketing piece. But instead writing responses, record yourself talking so the process feels more natural.

Dragon Dictation is a great tool for this task. The voice recognition application allows you to speak and instantly see your words as text. If you have an iPad or iPhone, the service is free.

Chapter 46

When Asking for Business is a Bad Idea

I recently gave a short seminar to a local business group about how to "sell" to today's skeptical consumers.

After my presentation, several people came up to me with marketing questions specific to their situations. One attendee's question, in particular, is especially worth sharing because it ties into a common mistake when marketing to prospects.

The guy provides consulting services to companies wanting to "improve overall business performance." He recently hung out his entrepreneurial shingle after retiring from a well-known global corporation.

Now he's on the hunt for clients.

His current marketing strategy involves targeting companies he wants to work with and then sending e-mails to contacts he finds online. The company he asked me about is one of the largest retail chains in the United States. And, unfortunately, he's frustrated because he can't get his message in front of the right decision-maker.

His disappointment is understandable ... and avoidable.

You see, he's making a mistake discussed in my book, *The "You" Effect: How to Transform Ego-Based Marketing Into Captivating Messages That Create Customers*:

You can't market effectively if you rely on interrupting as many people as possible with a message they never asked for.

The guy is essentially hoping to generate business by convincing people that they need his services. Worse yet, he is going about the process by pitching his services as an unknown source.

Sure, sometimes you should share your marketing message with people who haven't asked for it (especially if they already demonstrated desire for a product/service similar to yours). But asking for business as a way to introduce yourself is not an effective approach.

I encouraged the business owner to begin developing marketing materials that educate prospects about problems that hinder performance. That way he proves his position as an industry authority, instead of looking like just another person pitching services.

Furthermore, since he just started his business, I suggested first testing his message with smaller companies.

If the people you target don't realize they have the problem your product/service solves, trying to convince them to take action on your offer will almost always lead to frustration.

The convincing game is expensive and wastes your efforts. You're better off attracting prospects by sharing educational messages that develop relationships over time.

Chapter 47

5 Lies That Mess Up Your Marketing (and Cause You to Overspend)

When it comes to marketing, promises can be as plentiful as lies. Unfortunately, thanks to the Internet's far-reaching effects, almost anyone can attract an audience and spread misinformation.

So please excuse me as I hop atop the soapbox and shed light on five common claims.

Marketing Lie #1: *"People must see your ad 7 (or some higher number) times before they remember and respond to it."*

Truth: In my last book, *The "You" Effect*, I labeled this fib (likely created by a wishful ad exec) "the biggest lie in advertising." The reality is, prospects won't respond to a bad ad whether they see it once or 1,000 times. So keep adjusting your ad until it produces the leads you need. Expecting people to magically respond after a certain point is about as rational as believing in email's demise (see Lie #5).

Marketing Lie #2: *"You must get your company name and logo out there."*

Truth: Unless you're a big brand such as Amazon or Apple (and have a matching marketing budget), prospects couldn't care less about your company name or logo. So instead of making either the focal point in your marketing, prove your capabilities by delivering useful information that helps your prospects. After all, they only care about what you can do for them (even better if you can help them solve a problem).

Marketing Lie #3: *"We'll get you to page 1 on Google ... guaranteed."*

Truth: Getting your website listed on any search engine for a trivial phrase searched a few times each month won't bring you much benefit. Sure, some SEO trickery might help you ride higher in the results – but don't expect your "success" to last long. Of course, you can also use pay-per-click advertising for a top ranking. But, keep in mind, just because you have traffic doesn't mean those visitors convert and create sales.

Marketing Lie #4: *"I'll make you a best-selling author."*

"Best-selling author" is destined to become one of marketing's most meaningless phrases. These days, far too many authors with a title on an Amazon subcategory list have bestowed themselves as a "best seller." Please understand, Amazon best seller lists update every 60 minutes. Get several friends to buy your book at a specific time and you can sit atop an Amazon list for an hour or two. Have a Kindle version, spend a day giving it away for free and the "best seller" process becomes even easier.

Marketing Lie #5: *"Email is dead."*

Email's demise comes up every year. Thanks to social media and mobile devices, though, you could argue email is more alive than ever. After all, it allows for personal communication and relationship development when you establish yourself as a valued resource, instead of a self-promoting spammer. In fact, according to the Direct Marketing Association, email's current return on investment hovers around 4,300%. Not too bad for a "dead" medium.

Chapter 48

Why Eyeballs Don't Equal Attention

W hile reading *Sports Illustrated* recently, I came across a crazy example of copycat marketing.
Look at this:

The two ads are just 8 pages apart in the issue. According to SRDS (Standard Rate & Data Service), each full-page color spread cost a cool $370,500. Can you imagine approving this expense for such poor promotions?

Let's list a few problems right now …

No offer … no way to introduce prospects to the product … no call-to-action … no engagement opportunity … no way to measure response …

The similarities between the two ads make matters worse. Notice how each one uses the same layout and language. For example, one razor is described as a "shaving machine" and the other a "power tool."

Now, I don't know about you, but the thought of putting sharp, heavy-duty equipment near my face makes me flinch with fear!

Of course, Gillette and Schick are big brands. Both can afford to copy each other. But why not dare to be different?

My guess is these ads were designed to "build brand awareness" or "get the word out." Keep in mind, though, these objectives can't happen unless your marketing offers something that benefits your prospects.

Remember, eyeballs don't equal attention.

For $370,500, why not mail "shaving machines" to select SI subscribers? If people like the product, they must buy replacement blades, which immediately multiplies the return on your mailing investment.

When I turned 18, Gillette sent me a free Sensor in the mail and, until about a year ago, I bought replacement blades for it.

Why wouldn't a similar strategy work 20 years later?

Look, people don't seek out your marketing for enjoyment. You must interest them and make your message worth their time.

The reality is, too much marketing today just takes up space – and, in many cases, it's pricey real estate!

So what's different about your message?

Chapter 49

What to Do When Even Super Bowl-Sized Attention Can't Create Sales

I n what is far from a surprise in most direct-response marketing circles, the research firm Communicus recently released a study that showed 80% of Super Bowl ads end up selling squat.

Yep, advertisers spend up to $4 million for a 30-second spot and most see no increase in sales. In fact, the Tucson, Ariz.-based firm found about 60% of the ads it tested didn't even increase purchase intent.

Super Bowl commercials highlight one of the most over-glorified desires shared by entrepreneurs and executives who actively market their businesses – attention.

The fact is, attention alone can't create sales.

As we've discussed many times in this book, the most critical piece in the promotional puzzle is trust, which takes time and repeated contact to develop. Furthermore, effective marketing today involves interacting and delivering value to those who need your help.

In a Jan. 6, 2014, *Advertising Age* article, Communicus CEO Jeri Smith explained another big problem with Super Bowl commercials.

"The advertisers really dial up the entertainment quotient to pop to the top of the USA Today rankings and such," she said. "But we find the brand

association with Super Bowl commercials is much lower than you'd get with a typical buy, just because of the way the creative is structured."

Take a second or two and think back to last year's Super Bowl commercials. Which ones do you remember? Do you recall making a purchase because of something you saw on TV during the game?

According to the *USA Today Ad Meter*, Budweiser's baby Clydesdale spot was the most popular commercial during the 2013 Super Bowl. (Watch it here: http://youtu.be/uiJqzdOr4Ok.) Did you feel a sudden craving for a beer after you watched it?

Probably not … and you're not alone.

According to Anheuser-Busch, Budweiser's U.S. sales were down 4.1% during the first quarter of 2013. Nielsen also reported that Bud sales in the four weeks ending April 13 dropped 7.7%. (The game was played on Feb. 3, 2013.)

Of course, a Super Bowl commercial isn't the only factor that led to decreased sales. But what's important to note is that (again) attention alone doesn't cause consumers to open their wallets.

This is the primary reason why, instead of generating attention, I suggest concentrating your marketing efforts on creating relationships. Strategic invites are one way to handle this task.

In his *New York Times* best seller, *Book Yourself Solid: The Fastest, Easiest, and Most Reliable System for Getting More Clients Than You Can Handle – Even if You Hate Marketing and Selling*, Michael Port describes what he calls the "always-have-something-to-invite-people-to" offer.

The idea behind these offers is simple:

People generally hate to be sold, but they love to be invited – as long as the invitations are relevant and anticipated.

When Port first started his business, he offered a weekly teleseminar. Sometimes the topics covered ideas for getting more clients. Other times he shared strategies for becoming more successful in business and life.

Anyone could attend the calls for free. When he met people who might benefit from the information, he invited them to the next call. Eventually, the calls turned into an online social networking community.

He focused on adding value at all times. Of course, a percentage of his audience eventually became clients.

My sister-in-law is part of trio who use their Cincinnati-based company, Cooking with Caitlin, to "inspire culinary confidence." About five years ago, the three ladies organized their invite offer using Twitter.

Now, every Monday from 5-6:30 p.m. EST, foodies flock to the social networking service to share tips and ideas using the hashtag #FNIchat. The 90-minute online party averages between 100-200 active participants, resulting in about 1,000 unique lines of communication and 3-5 million potential impressions.

The event that began as a way to bring together food fans is so popular now that it attracts sponsorships from big brands such as Hellmann's, Sun Chips and Kraft.

For me, I continue to fall back on free reports as my invite offer, and I then communicate with these communities often (mostly through email). Recently, I also started giving more attention to my Marketing Minds Podcast and its iTunes audience.

Regardless of what medium or method you choose for your free invite offer, don't skimp on value.

"Please give away so much value that you think you've given too much, and then give more," Port emphasizes.

Not only does this approach establish you as a helpful resource, it also builds your credibility and likeability. What's more, you leverage your time because you connect with many potential clients at once.

Chapter 50

A Complete Copywriting Course in a Single Sentence

Does the name Frederick Buechner ring a bell with you? He is an American writer and theologian who has penned 36 published books. Described as "one of our most original storytellers" by *USA Today*, Beuchner has also been a Pulitzer Prize finalist.

And although his work primarily involves fiction, autobiographies, essays and sermons, I can't help but think the 87-year-old would be an incredible copywriter for marketing materials.

What's crazy is I make this assessment based on merely 16 words he's credited with saying. Essentially, the words serve as a complete copywriting course in a single sentence ...

"They may forget what you said, but they will never forget how you made them feel."

You may want to read that quote again. The advice is critical to creating effective marketing materials.

You see, not enough marketing pieces incorporate feelings – a silly oversight, especially when you realize emotions are the foundation for all buying decisions. Instead, most marketing touts items such as experience, customer service and capabilities.

Again, you miss opportunities when you limit your message to these "givens."

So what emotional triggers can you tie into your marketing message?

Is fear a possibility? What about anger, guilt or gratification? Or how about a desire to belong, a yearning for more time or a need to keep up with the Joneses?

Please take 30 seconds and read the following advertisement:

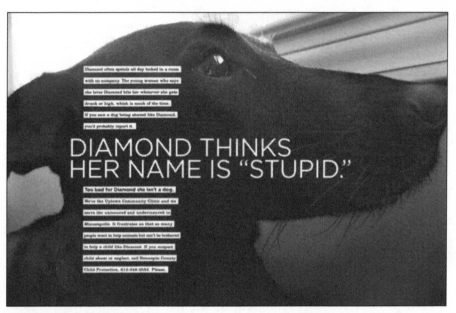

Source: Ads of the World

Okay, now how do you feel?

I suspect the anger or sadness you sense didn't exist a minute ago.

Of course, if the organization in the ad followed a "traditional" approach, you would know all their services, details about their decades of experience and their unwavering commitment to kids.

But then does this information make the ad memorable?

Absolutely not.

Chapter 51

Why Specifics Sell and Generalities Fail

T he most dependable way to generate leads from your marketing is by telling prospects what you can do for them in exchange for their hard-earned cash.

Now, you may think this concept is common sense. But it's ignored all the time in marketing materials.

Let me explain ...

I love picking through the mail. Almost every day I sort through the letters, bills and ads that splash across our living room floor the moment the mailman walks off our front porch. We have one of those old mail slots next to the front door, so you immediately know when the mail arrives.

Anyway, it's rare when I see a company tell me specifically what it will do for my money. Most times the messages simply state a company name and the product or service it provides.

For example, I often see postcards with messages such as ...

Franklin Auto Shop. Come see us for your next oil change.

You might then see a phone number or website.

Sure, the above message might tell you what the company does – and even provide a price. But what do you *really* get for your money?

You see, vague messages don't sell as well as specific statements.

Notice the specifics in the following example from Oil Can Henry's "Famous 20-Point Full-Service Oil Change":

Our Famous 20-Point Full-Service Oil Change is preventative maintenance that helps ensure your vehicle is operating safely and efficiently.

It's easy, too! You just relax in the comfort of your car as we perform the oil change and complete a thorough review of your vehicle's recommended services, as determined by the manufacturer.

Each oil change also comes with Henry's Top-Up Guarantee: If your vehicle is low on any fluid within three months of your last Oil Can Henry's service, go to any Oil Can Henry's service center, present the receipt from your last service and we'll "top-up" the fluid to its proper level at no charge.

Note: For your safety, we do not top-up brake fluid.

Our Famous 20-Point Full-Service Oil Change includes:

New Oil*	*Wash Windshield*
New Oil Filter	*Under Hood Visual Inspection*
Lubricate Chassis	*Under Chassis Visual Inspection*

CHECK AND FILL:

Power Steering Fluid	*Transfer Case*
Battery	*Radiator Coolant Recovery Level*
Transmission/Transaxle	*Windshield Washer Fluid*
Differential (Front and Rear)	*Tire Pressure*

CHECK AND INSPECT:

Brake Fluid	*PCV Valve*
Air Filter	*Lights*
Crankcase Breather (PCV Filter)	*Windshield Wipers*

Keep in mind, it's likely many other auto shops provide these same services with an oil change. But few ever share the information in their marketing materials.

In my book, *The Reluctant Writer's Guide to Creating Powerful Marketing Materials: 61 Easy Ideas to Attract Attention and Create More Customers*, I tell the story of how – more than 80 years ago – advertising writer Claude Hopkins overcame the challenge of marketing a product identical to many competitors.

His client was Schlitz and the product was beer. At the time, Schlitz held fifth place in its industry. The strategy you're about to read propelled the Milwaukee brewer into a tie for first after only a few months.

Schlitz's rise to prominence has been called the greatest success in beer advertising. Not only do you see beer's biggest brands using the same strategy today, but it's also something you can apply to any business.

When Hopkins began studying other beer companies, he noticed they all announced the same claim in their advertising –"pure." In his book, *My Life in Advertising*, Hopkins explained how brewers would publicize the word in big letters. Some would even buy double-page ads so "pure" was displayed as large as possible.

Hopkins recognized the claim had little effect on prospects. So he went to a Schlitz brewery in search of a solution.

Once there, he saw plate-glass rooms filled with filtered air where beer dripped over pipes. The process allowed the beer to cool in purity.

Next, he saw large filters packed with white-wood pulp, and then watched how every pump and pipe was cleaned twice daily to avoid contamination. Even the bottles were washed four times by machinery.

Although the brewery sat on the shores of Lake Michigan, Hopkins saw how Schlitz tapped artesian wells to collect pure water from 4,000 feet below the ground. He was also shown vats where beer aged for six months before it went to users.

A stop in the laboratory revealed how the yeast used in Schlitz beer was developed from an original cell that required 1,200 experiments before the finest taste was discovered.

Once back at the office, Hopkins asked, *"Why don't you tell people these things? Why do you merely try to cry louder than others that your beer is pure? Why don't you tell the reasons?"*

"Why?" was the response. *"The processes we use are just the same as others use. No one can make good beer without them."*

Hopkins had a hunch people would respond to reading how Schlitz achieved "pure" beer. So he used print ads (see above) to tell stories that gave purity meaning.

Notice how Hopkins supported his claims with specific facts and didn't assume prospects knew information his client believed was common knowledge. Too often, we're so close to our companies that it's difficult to realize what prospects truly understand.

Also, Hopkins was a master at educating his readers. When you walk away from reading one of his ads, you feel a little wiser.

And, finally, Hopkins wasn't hesitant about using long copy. He understood prospects crave as much information as possible before making a purchase. After all, who would ever handicap a salesman by only allowing him to speak a certain number of words?

Chapter 52

How to Make Your Mark by Creating a Loyal Following

C ontroversy shook the whiskey world in 2013.
But unless you're a devoted whiskey drinker or live close to Loretto, Kentucky, you probably didn't notice the news.

Maker's Mark, a company with a fiercely loyal following, announced it was lowering the alcohol content of its whiskey due to overwhelming demand.

You see, making a batch of Maker's Mark takes at least six years. So diluting existing reserves is the fastest way to increase supply.

The decision triggered an instant uproar, especially on social media. After all, Maker's Mark execs essentially admitted they would soon offer a lower-quality product.

Then, about a week later, CEO Rob Samuels and Chairman Emeritus Bill Samuels, Jr. announced via a link on Twitter, "We are reversing our decision to lower the ABV of Maker's Mark, and resuming production at 45% alcohol by volume (90 proof)."

For the most part, the media attacked Maker's Mark management for its foolishness. But I still believe, besides deciding to water down its whiskey (and not embracing the scarcity and social proof the situation offered), the company makes many smart moves that business owners/entrepreneurs can learn from and incorporate into their marketing efforts.

First, it's worth noting that the dilution decision was initially announced to Maker's Mark Ambassadors, an all-volunteer group that fuels the company's marketing engine. As official card-carrying members, these company advocates receive gifts to help spread the Maker's Mark message.

(The promotional items – such as bottle sweaters, gift boxes/wrap and stickers – are so popular that people auction them off on eBay! Can you imagine a company's marketing materials so in demand that customers sell them?)

As an Ambassador, you also get your name engraved on a barrel of aging bourbon, an opportunity to buy a bottle of Maker's Mark from "your" batch (when it's ready), updates on the aging of your bourbon, invites to exclusive events, and several nomination cards to recommend others for the group.

In effect, your Ambassador status gives you a level of ownership in the company – and membership doesn't cost you a single cent.

Brilliant!

Keep in mind, Maker's Mark does not promote its Ambassador program. Advertisements never mention it. In-store displays don't show it. And on the website, you need patience and a little luck to uncover the registration page.

Maker's Mark also won't reveal how many members are in the group. But the count likely reaches well into the thousands. (A Maker's Mark Ambassadors group on Facebook alone has more than 10,000 members.)

Pretty impressive, isn't it?

In addition to regular communication with Ambassadors through snail mail, the company is active via e-mail and social media.

These conversations involve people who want to hear from Maker's Mark – not an interrupted audience that hasn't asked for communication from the company (as is the case with most marketing messages).

Ambassadors are treated as friends. They receive behind-the-scenes access to company operations … sneak peeks at new products … and, in general, communication that makes them feel special.

The result is incredible loyalty.

Furthermore, just as if from a friend or family member, e-mails from Maker's Mark come to Ambassadors in text format. There are no fancy graphics, dull templates or exaggerated logos, as are common with most companies' e-mail communication.

The relationships created by Maker's Mark marketing even carry over to the Ambassadors themselves. After your name is added to a barrel at the company's distillery, you receive photo proof and then opportunities to communicate with your other 29 barrel mates.

Now, I'm not an Ambassador (I interviewed several for this chapter), but I think we can assume the primary conversation topic isn't the weather. They, of course, chat about whiskey (and, in all likelihood, Maker's Mark).

Unfortunately, rarely do businesses apply a fraction of the effort Marker's Mark does in creating loyalty and an audience of advocates. The marketing attention instead revolves around creating instant sales, especially when leads dry up.

Remember, your marketing must develop relationships before it can drive profits.

So when was the last time you communicated with your prospects and clients for a reason other than pitching your product or service?

Chapter 53

How to Convert a Commodity Into an Experience That Brings You Buyers

T he Oct. 29, 2013, *Washington Post* headline read like a warning ...

Small business owners fear shutdown's aftershocks will hurt holiday sales

This title is the latest in what's become relentless coverage of struggles within the small-business community.

"News" like this drives me nuts – and I'm sure I'm not alone.

The media continues to toss around business problems, blame and excuses like water bottles at a Justin Bieber concert (check TMZ if you don't understand the reference).

The article states: *"In the immediate aftermath of the 17-day shutdown, just 13 percent of small-business owners polled on Oct. 18 said they were more optimistic about sales this season,* **while 43 percent said they expected sales to drop during the holidays**. *Meanwhile, half specifically said they expect the fallout from the government shutdown will prompt shoppers to spend less than they would have to close out the year."*

So do business owners and entrepreneurs really allow these doom-and-gloom predictions to affect their mindset and marketing approach?

Without a doubt ... YES!

Earlier this year, I came across a CNN article that chronicled the struggles of a shoe salesman in New York City. The man, Nelson Springer, works for Macy's and is frustrated because his commissions keep getting smaller due to shoppers buying shoes online.

Since his situation is so common nowadays, I couldn't help but contact CNN with an offer to help.

You see, if you look at Springer's situation (or any brick-and-mortar business with online competition) from a traditional sales perspective, there are only two ways to boost profits:

1.   Get more customers to buy stuff

2.   Raise prices

Unfortunately for Springer, neither is a viable option. As the article explained, he's already trying to sell more shoes. But the appeal of shopping online overshadows his efforts. And second, he has no control over the prices Macy's puts on their footwear.

So what's left for a commission-dependent salesman to do? What about a business owner or entrepreneur hassled by lower prices at other places?

Plenty.

First, anyone in this situation would benefit by avoiding the "salesman" label – whether it's part of the job or perceived by prospects. The title alone implies your sole purpose is selling.

When you're seen as a salesman, you force prospects to use a single variable when deciding whether to buy from you – price. Your product instantly becomes a commodity because price is the only way to distinguish your offer from similar alternatives.

In Springer's case, I suggest he begin presenting himself as an authority on all things shoes. He likely already shares his shoe knowledge with customers. Now take that insight and deliver it in a shareable format.

Maybe he offers customers a printed guide on how to pick the proper dress shoes (and provides tips for different occasions) ... or records video reviews of new arrivals ... or creates tutorials on making shoes last longer ... or interviews representatives from the shoe brands offered by Macy's ... or writes articles about mistakes to avoid when shopping for shoes ...

Besides giving away this information in person, Springer can share it with new (and larger) audiences by posting on a blog, YouTube, iTunes, Facebook, Twitter and other media.

These actions (and the added frequency) would help establish Springer as a recognized authority and a helpful resource – rather than just another person selling shoes. Furthermore, his online educational material plays right into shoppers' evolving buying habits.

Of course, Springer should also distribute his information "products" to past customers. That is, assuming he collects contact information during purchases – which he should.

And speaking of customers ...

Why not regularly alert them to new offers (in addition to sharing helpful shoe-related information)? Or send e-mails when updated versions of previously purchased shoes become available?

In many cases, past customers stop spending only because they aren't given more opportunities to buy.

Remember, trust is already established with past customers. So it takes less effort to get them to buy again. On the other hand, attracting new customers requires more effort and resources because trust isn't developed yet.

Make sense?

Let's also not overlook ways Springer can get customers to spend more. He can simply offer other goods (and even services) with his shoes. Socks, belts and shirts are easy options. Some type of shoe maintenance plan is even a possibility.

Thanks to Springer's employer, finding and storing extra inventory isn't a problem. All sorts of complementary products already sit on store shelves.

He could even package products with pairs of shoes to create higher ticket items. Shoppers benefit from convenience because they get everything at once, instead of waiting for separate online shipments.

Of course, once Nelson's authority status grows, consulting is another money-making option. After all, he's in New York City where many view fashion and style like a religion. There's also a large corporate audience that could seek out shoe and/or fashion advice.

And, finally, don't forget joint ventures and referral sources. Partnerships with local suit tailors, shoe shines and even doctors are possibilities.

So what have I missed? What ideas can you think of for dealing with a situation like Nelson's?

Chapter 54

The Fastest Way to Turn Your Business Into an Ignored Commodity

A big price battle started brewing just before Christmas last year. Target announced year-round price matching of online retailers – such as Amazon.com, Walmart.com, BestBuy.com and Toysrus. com – in all its stores.

This new policy is designed to curb "showrooming," the practice of examining merchandise inside a store and then buying the same product online at a lower price.

As smartphone use and mobile shopping increases, showrooming becomes a bigger headache for brick-and-mortar retailers. Apps such as RedLaser further complicate matters by allowing shoppers to scan a product's barcode and instantly see pricing options online and at other local retailers.

You can't blame Target for addressing the problem. However, the announcement puts the discount retailer in a dangerous position, as it tries to catch up to the online shopping heavyweights (especially Amazon.com).

Target's problem begs the question ...

Should you match competitors' pricing?

Before you do, remember, price is only one factor prospects consider when buying. Sure, deals sometimes come in the form of cheap prices.

However, you can also deliver deals by bundling items, providing extra services, creating experiences, offering unexpected perks, or just sharing helpful advice. **As a business owner or entrepreneur, you must prove to prospects that they're getting great value – not just a great price.**

When what you offer becomes indistinguishable from others and clients buy only on price, your business becomes a commodity.

Look at Starbucks. Coffee is a commodity, but Starbucks turned buying it into a multisensory experience.

You smell the aroma when you walk in ... you see the inviting environment ... you hear the sounds of conversations and clicking keyboards ... you can touch coffee-related merchandise ... and, of course, there's the taste of your $5 customized latte.

This all combines to create an experience you can't replicate by buying coffee beans off your supermarket shelf.

Apple achieved similar success selling personal computers (and related electronic devices).

Nordstrom did the same with clothing and accessories. Even the neighborhood ice cream shop that my kids love like a family member has avoided commoditization.

The bottom line: If your prospects can't see your value, differentiate your offer and understand what you bring to the table, you're allowing them to commoditize your business.

Chapter 55

4 Factors That Determine Consumer Buyer Behavior

Apple is often seen as the poster child for business brilliance. The company rarely makes a wrong move. Major media devotes extensive coverage to every new product. And Apple fans are arguably the most loyal of any brand in the business world.

That's why it's interesting to see Apple's response to actions from what some see as the company's primary competition in the smartphone market – Samsung.

From a marketing perspective, both sides know their audiences and target them well. This is a major difference from many business owners and entrepreneurs who mistakenly market as if anyone with a wallet is a valid prospect.

In one of its latest commercials, Samsung, for example, seeks to push away the status-seeking crowd often associated with Apple products. In fact, the company blatantly alienates a huge audience.

Is this a smart move?

Well, I'm not a fan of attack tactics. But I understand the reasoning behind Samsung's strategy. The company's marketing staff recognizes that many of their prospects see themselves among an anti-Apple crowd.

Now, I'm not here to decide whether or not Samsung's tactics sell more smartphones. Instead, the lesson worth noting from both companies is the importance of who you target with your marketing.

Keep in mind, prospects buy products and services for four basic reasons – they either need, want, wish or desire what you offer.

For example, a prospect may buy a criminal defense attorney's services because he *needs* help after getting arrested for a violent crime. He may buy a Toyota Prius because *wants* to make a strong statement about his environmental beliefs. He may buy a larger house because he *wishes* to "keep up with the Joneses." Or he may buy a high-powered speed boat because he *desires* the attention it attracts while skimming across the lake.

As you can see, there's a purpose for every purchase. And it's this purpose that drives the sale – not the product or service.

So what motivates your prospects to take action? What are their biggest needs, wants, wishes or desires?

What problems or frustrations keep your prospect from achieving this outcome?

Once you incorporate the reasons behind people's purchases into your marketing, you increase the odds of getting greater responses.

Chapter 56

The Biggest Lie in Advertising

Recently, while helping a new client fix an underperforming ad, I was reminded of several advertising myths and one especially large lie that ad execs often drop on unsuspecting business owners and entrepreneurs.

This fib is likely responsible for millions of dollars in unnecessary spending. Of course, ad execs don't want anyone spilling the beans on their dirty little secret. But you need to know the truth.

If you've done any print advertising, you've likely heard the following statement:

Readers must see your ad multiple times before they remember and respond to it.

Please, from now on, ignore this advice when you hear it. The ad execs only tell you this to pad their pockets. The truth is …

If you run a bad ad, you won't get responses whether you run it 1 or 1,000 times. An ineffective ad can't magically become effective, regardless of how many times you use it.

Listen, both my kids hate eating spinach. If I put a plate of the green leafy stuff in front of them tonight, they won't touch it. If I serve the same plate tomorrow … the following day … the next 30 days … or even every day for the next year, I'll get the same response.

Your ad is no different.

That's why it's critical you make changes to your ads until they generate the leads you need. If a publication insists you run the same ad over and over again, stop advertising with them.

When I started with the client mentioned earlier, the newspaper's printing deadline made it impossible for us to incorporate even a fraction of my recommended changes. Therefore, the only text we could adjust was the headline.

So what happened?

The ad generated seven leads the first time it ran. Again, all we changed was the headline.

The previous weeks the ad ran it only brought in two leads – total.

We boosted response in later weeks by making two more changes. First, I encouraged the client to run a smaller ad because he previously used a full-page spread. I also recommended he stop using color and move to black and white.

You see, a bigger ad doesn't necessarily generate more leads – and neither does color. The smart approach to advertising is to start small. Then, as your ad generates leads, you use the added revenue to move up sizes or test color.

Any other approach only wastes money.

Chapter 57

How to Quickly Qualify Prospects With Your Copy

E ver see an ad while searching the Internet and then notice it follows you to other sites like a lost puppy?

For several years, I've watched an ad run online with virtually the same copy. The only adjustments have been an occasional headline or image change.

Now, for an ad junkie like me, I love when this happens. The reason is simple:

When you see an ad run relatively unchanged for a long period of time (especially in heavily circulated publications), you can often assume it's generating consistent leads. After all, a smart business owner or entrepreneur won't continue paying for an ad that doesn't work.

The ad I keep seeing is from Fisher Investments. Here's one version:

During the most recent presidential election, headline variations read, *What Would Happen to the Stock Market if Barack Obama is Re-Elected?* or *What Would Happen to the Stock Market if Mitt Romney is Elected?* These adjustments are great examples of tying your ad into current events.

However, for the sake of this chapter's tip, I want you to notice the first sentence in the body copy. Fisher Investments uses one of my favorite fill-in-the-blank formulas for capturing control of readers' eyeballs and luring them deeper into your copy. The strategy also instantly pre-qualifies prospects.

Here's the formula: *If (insert your prospect's problem(s) or desired result(s)), then (insert your bold promise).*

In the case of the Fisher Investments ad, instead of a problem or result as a "qualifying" item, an achievement is used.

The above formula is effective because our brains are biologically programmed to follow the logic of "if/then" statements. As a result, your prospects are more willing to accept your written words as truth, even before you present evidence.

So if I wrote an if/then statement to introduce this article, I might say ...

If you need an easy way to dodge your prospects' inner critic and write a marketing message that's practically impossible to resist, then the few minutes you spend reading this article will be the most valuable time investment you make all day.

Pretty easy stuff, right?

Well, here's another copy secret that, in addition to qualifying your prospects, can help you overcome the mind's natural defense mechanism.

First, understand that the mind doesn't welcome change. Instant rejection is much more common than acceptance. This decision process occurs fast and often without conscious control.

The moment your marketing message contains an idea your prospects' minds can't accept, any thought of making a purchase is rejected and your opportunity is lost forever. But when your copy can switch off the brain's critical component, you give your marketing message a fighting chance of getting evaluated.

One way to temporarily disable your prospects' inner critic is by calling attention to specific problems. After all, problems are "messages" your mind can relate to because you actively think about them.

Let me give you an example.

A few years ago, when promoting a new special report, *Marketing Materials Made Easy: 8 Secrets for Attracting Attention, Creating Customers and Building Your Business*, I targeted certain prospects with the following phrase:

For business owners and professionals fed up by the lack of leads generated by their company's marketing materials – and can't figure out what's wrong …

Notice how I don't just target "business owners" or "professionals." What good would it do me to pursue such a general group?

Instead, I want business owners and professionals who are concerned about their marketing materials … frustrated because their promotional efforts are failing … and confused about what can be done to generate leads. Once I have the attention of these targeted prospects, I can then pile on reasons for needing my special report.

You can use this same approach in any industry. So let's say you're a criminal defense lawyer in Chicago. You might use:

For Chicago residents accused of a violent crime who feel overwhelmed with decisions, confused about legal options and scared about their future – and can't figure out where to turn for honest advice …

Now check out the ad below. Notice how Fisher Investments also uses a similar approach in the headline – and the ad is just a variation of the one shown earlier.

Ads by Google

To investors who want to retire comfortably.

If you have a $500,000 portfolio, download the guide written by *Forbes* columnist and money manager Ken Fisher's firm. It's called "**The 15-Minute Retirement Plan.**" Even if you have something else in place right now, it *still* makes sense to request your guide!

Click Here to Download Your Guide!

Fisher Investments®

Don't wait to try these two tips in your next marketing piece. I'd love to hear how they work for you.

Chapter 58

The 8 Items That Make 'Dangerous' Ads Deliver Leads

I'm a sucker for the stories behind successful advertisements. For example, ever hear of Ernest Shackleton? He was an Irish-born, 20th century explorer who led numerous polar expeditions and devoted his life to one goal:

Complete the first crossing of Antarctica.

In 1901, he came within 745 miles of the South Pole. Seven years later, he pressed to within just 97 miles.

Then, in 1914, he coordinated what was billed as the *British Imperial Trans-Antarctic Expedition*. But before he could set sail, he needed a crew.

So, as records show, he placed an ad for recruits in a London newspaper. It read:

MEN WANTED
for hazardous journey, small wages,
bitter cold, long months of complete
darkness, constant danger, safe return doubtful, honor and recognition
in case of success.

Ernest Shackleton 4 Burlington st.

Crazy ad, isn't it? After all, who would volunteer for such torture?

Well, the ad resulted in more than 5,000 men applying for the "job." Of those people, Shackleton selected 27 for his crew.

I tell you this story because it demonstrates someone who didn't hesitate to promote in a daring way.

Of course, you don't have to go this extreme. But you do have to be different if you expect to stand out from your competitors.

When you market in an unconventional manner, you'll feel alone at times. People will criticize you.

And that's okay.

In Shackleton's case, his journey created incredible hardship that delivered on the ad's promise. His wooden ship (appropriately named *Endurance*) became trapped in pack ice.

Eventually, after nearly two years of drifting on ice flows, settling on an uninhabited island, and crossing 26 miles of mountains and gla-ciers to reach a whaling station, he led all 27 members of his crew to rescue.

Shackleton's journey and the promotion around it were dan-gerous. Unfortunately, this same term is typically used by busi-ness owners and entrepreneurs when considering marketing that's different.

Sure, failure is possible when going against the norm. After all, like Shackleton, you're exploring unfamiliar waters. So if Plan A doesn't work, simply start testing other options.

When advertising, I use an 8-point checklist to help determine if an ad is different enough to attract attention and generate responses. Here are the requirements:

1. Would this piece attract attention if positioned near competitors (is it better than the ordinary)?

2. Does this piece avoid the appearance of being an ad?

3. Is the message focused on the prospect, instead of the business?

4. Is the piece too valuable to throw away?

5. Does the piece have a headline that lures in prospects?

6. Does the piece target a single audience?

7. Does the copy "talk" in a casual language prospects understand?

8. Does the piece have a compelling offer that makes the next step crystal clear?

To conclude, let me refer to history again and leave you with a quote from mid-1900s English photographer and artist Sir Cecil Beaton:

"Be daring, be different, be impractical, be anything that will assert integrity of purpose and imaginative vision against the play-it-safers, the creatures of the commonplace, the slaves of the ordinary."

Chapter 59

11 Ways to Correct Your Copy and Boost Response

Copy Correction #1: "Speak" your prospects' language. Readers will understand your copy better if you use simple words with clear concepts. So don't be afraid to write casually. Not only can you still sound professional using basic language, but your copy won't read like it was created by a corporate machine.

Copy Correction #2: State the problem you help your prospects' solve. When you match your copy the way your prospects describe their problem, you're in a powerful position because you zero in on thoughts already in their minds. After all, when an issue causes you stress, you can't stop thinking about it, right?

And, because your prospects are already pondering a problem, it's easier to bypass the brain's natural reaction to reject new ideas.

Copy Correction #3: Address beliefs and emotions your prospects have about their situation. Common thoughts shape your prospects' attitudes about the solution you offer. They may believe your solution is too expensive … you don't have enough experience … you're too busy to help … you'll pressure them with a sales pitch at the first opportunity …

As for their problem, maybe they believe it's too complicated for a quick solution … requires resources they can't access … involves issues no one else has experienced … entails dealing with topics they're too embarrassed to discuss …

In addition, are your prospects frustrated, scared or confused? Do they feel guilty? Are they insecure about their situation?

Whatever your prospects' beliefs and emotions, address these concerns or you risk losing their attention.

Copy Correction #4: Focus on the outcome delivered by your product or service. Your prospects don't want your product or service. Instead, they want the outcome it provides.

So if you're a portrait photographer, your prospects don't want you to take pictures – they want visual memories they can't wait to share with friends and family. If you're a criminal defense lawyer, a guy just pulled over for extreme DUI doesn't want legal representation – he wants to stay out of jail, get his record cleared and have a chance at living a normal life again.

Use your copy to provide insight that puts prospects closer to their desired outcome.

Copy Correction #5: Question your readers. One easy way to trigger mental dialogue is with one- or two-word questions. This practice enhances your copy because it mimics the way we talk.

Basically, you write a statement and then give your reader an opportunity to take in the idea by asking a question. Some of my favorite questions include "Make sense?" "Right?" "Understand?" "Fair enough?" and "Sound familiar?"

Notice the question at the end of this letter intro for a tax attorney (you'll see I also addressed prospects' emotions):

Catching up with the IRS on your offshore bank account probably isn't a topic you're eager to discuss – and that's okay.

If you're like others in your situation, you're feeling confused, scared and maybe even embarrassed. Keep in mind, these emotions are natural …

You're not alone.

Of course, you'd prefer the issue just go away, right? Realistically, though, you know that won't happen, which is why you sought out this information.

Copy Correction #6: Command your reader's mental involvement. Another conversational copy technique is inserting command statements at the beginning of sentences. Some of my favorites are "listen," "remember," "keep in mind" and "imagine."
For instance …

Keep in mind, when you don't grab control of your 401k or at least educate yourself about your investment options, you limit your retirement to what the market delivers.

You can also use longer command statements as transitions. Here are several examples:

Allow me to explain …

Listen to this story …

Let's take a look at what I'm talking about …

Think about that for a minute …

And here's one fact you can't ignore …

Copy Correction #7: Explain the "because." People seek reasons for taking action when you ask them to do something. The word "because" acts as a trigger. It not only tells your prospects why they should comply, but also increases the likelihood they will take action.

Copy Correction #8: Provide proof. Without evidence, solutions become empty words stealing space in your marketing materials. Remember, your prospects are skeptical. Show them you're credible and prove what you offer is legit by incorporating testimonials, case studies, references to research, comparisons or a guarantee.

Copy Correction #9: Tell a story. Stories are powerful persuasion tools that can help you generate sales because they allow readers to form their own conclusions. People are drawn to stories – they have a natural desire to relate to the characters.

In every company, on every day, people (including you) overcome adversity, solve problems and deliver results. Explain these experiences in stories.

One of the easiest ways to write a sales-generating story is by explaining how a client successfully used your product or service. Start by simply writing down the facts you want to highlight. Then fill in the gaps by explaining the problem, the action taken and the results achieved.

Copy Correction #10: Use italics, bold and underlines to occasionally highlight information essential to your message. The way your prospects read your copy can create unintended meanings. So you must clarify important points.

For example, check out the following exercise from legendary sales trainer Zig Ziglar. Read each sentence and put extra emphasis on the italicized word. Notice how the meaning of each sentence changes.

I didn't say she stole the money.
I *didn't* say she stole the money.
I didn't *say* she stole the money.
I didn't say *she* stole the money.
I didn't say she *stole* the money.
I didn't say she stole the *money.*

Copy Correction #11: Deliver value. What would you do if you could only put one marketing piece in front of the leads you gathered this week? How would you approach those prospects? Would the copy you present to them be the same you use today?

Would you rely on pitching your product or service – or would you venture along another route?

Before you make your decision, consider this final thought:

You'll never go wrong in your marketing (which includes your copy) when you show compassion and a desire for helping people.

Chapter 60

Break These 'Rules' to Write More Memorable Marketing Copy

I cringed the moment my eyes saw the following instructions on my daughter's homework:

Circle the correct helping verb in each sentence.

The page then featured a list of sentences ...

1) *I (is, am, are) working on my science fair project.*

2) *I (do, does, did) go to Disneyland last year.*

3) *Carlos and Jamal (is, are) arguing about the game.*

4) *My friend (have, has, had) already left for school when I called.*

5) *My brother (is, am, are) going to be six years old tomorrow.*

6) *I (have, has, had) to wash the dishes before I can go.*

7) *Jessica (have, has) always gotten good grades.*

8) *We (is, am, are) playing softball on Saturday.*

9) *Marcus (was, were) mowing the lawn when I got there.*

10) *Mandy (do, does) want to volunteer for the fundraiser.*

At first glance, you might think this exercise seems harmless.

The problem, however, is helping verbs act like copy kryptonite when marketing. They weaken your words and make proper comprehension difficult.

They also create unnecessary wordiness.

Now, don't get me wrong. You need helping verbs in some instances. But, for the most part, use the following 23 copy killers sparingly:

- being
- be
- am
- is
- are
- was
- were
- been
- have
- has
- had
- do
- does
- did
- can
- could
- will
- would
- shall
- should
- may
- might
- must

So let's look at how we might adjust a few of the earlier sentences.

2) I flew to Disneyland last year.
3) Carlos and Jamal keep arguing about the game.
7) Jessica always earns good grades.
Did you notice the stronger verbs?

Of course, these changes also tie into writing in the active voice, or constructing sentences where the subject "acts."

If you ever took a writing course, you may remember hearing this advice before. Sentences written in active voice have action and directness, which helps lure readers deeper into your copy.

Two common words that lead to passive sentences include "was" and "by."

So instead of *"The advertisement was written by me,"* you might write *"I wrote the advertisement."*

Just like with active verbs, writing in the active voice isn't necessary all the time. In fact, even in *Elements of Style* (long considered the Bible of English grammar), co-author William Strunk, Jr. states, "This rule does not, of course, mean that the writer should entirely discard the passive voice, which is frequently convenient and sometimes necessary."

Keep in mind, the copy that best connects with prospects is conversational. When read aloud, it sounds like a discussion with a friend over lunch.

Unfortunately, most people don't write the way they talk. Instead, they turn to the formal tone taught by high school English teachers. The result is a stiff, boring style that isn't easy to read or remember.

Conversational copy uses short words (and sentences) … repeated information … occasional questions … and causal pauses …

You also engage one person – not a large audience. And the dialog goes back and forth.

Of course, if you haven't used this type of copy in your marketing before, it might seem odd at first. You may feel uncomfortable even trying to write it.

Don't worry, though. Your natural voice will eventually come through after a little practice. If you continue having trouble, record yourself telling someone about your product or service. Then transcribe the recording.

Chapter 61

How to Get World-Class Authorities to Solve Your Most Pressing Problems

Marketing consultant Graham McGregor released a report in 2013 with a survey that sheds light on what people worry about most.

Here's a quick rundown:

- 40% of what people worry about never happens.

- 30% of what people worry about already happened – so you can't do anything about it.

- 12% of what the average person worries about is what others say about them – which, as we know, often isn't true.

- And, finally, 10% of survey respondents' worries dealt with health – which only makes your well-being worse, right?

That leaves just 8% of worries you could consider "real" problems. But does worrying ever really do any good in these situations?

The point is, we worry about far too many problems that won't happen or already occurred. This is wasted energy you can direct toward taking action.

Listen, I bet you have an area in your business where you desire improvement. This same area is also likely a source of stress.

Am I right?

Well, I'm about to give you a 30-day challenge so you can eliminate this tension. But first, let's dig in to your desired improvement.

When you want results in a certain area of your business, an idea is usually the obstacle holding you back. You're either hoping for a "light bulb" moment or guidance from someone who already achieved your desired result.

Fortunately, the ideas you need are everywhere. In fact, you know where to find them.

The Internet makes identifying well-known experts in areas where you desire improvement easy. So start familiarizing yourself with these people today.

Maybe you begin by reading an article or two from that person. Then you move on to a few presentations. You may even want to hire the person for advice.

(Yes, I know this challenge seems obvious. But obvious actions are often ignored actions.)

Now, let's take this challenge a step further ...

Did you know there's a super simple way to get experts' most valuable advice without ever hiring them? In fact, this overlooked opportunity causes even the most well-known authorities to spill their best success secrets.

This strategy is ...

The interview.

When people know they're "on record" (whether in print, audio or video format), their mentality shifts. They make sure they sound knowledgeable and portray a positive impression, especially when an audience is involved.

Look at Oprah. She used interviews to build her business empire. Who says you can't apply Oprah's approach to your business – just on a smaller scale?

Once you have your target authority, simply request an interview.

McGregor used interviews to create a free 396-page e-book called *The Unfair Business Advantage Report*. It contains insight from 32 top sales and marketing experts from five countries. Each expert shared their best strategy for boosting profits, increasing sales and creating an "unfair" business advantage.

The entire report is transcribed interviews. You can download it for free at www.TheUnfairBusinessAdvantage.com.

In the marketing world, two other people who use the interview strategy well are Joseph Bushnell at WebMarketingInnerCircle.com and David Siteman Garland from www.TheRiseToTheTop.com. While they have different approaches, both secure incredible interviews with the biggest names in business. I encourage you to check out their work.

Now, for your challenge ...

Target a single improvement area in your business for the next 30 days. Then determine the obstacle holding you back.

Next, find 1-3 people who overcame the obstacle and achieved your desired outcome. After you spend time familiarizing yourself with their work, set up a time to interview at least one of these people.

Here's What to Do Next ...

The strategies revealed in this book work. In fact, now that you know how to market in a way that builds trust, you'll begin noticing these ideas in action.

You now have a choice. There's no reason you can't succeed at elevating your marketing above the promotional garbage dumped on us every day. All you need is the desire to do something different and escape the expected.

So what's holding you back?

You just invested your most valuable asset – time – reading this book. Your decisions after closing the cover will determine your return on that investment.

Imagine what's possible with the new weapons in your marketing arsenal ...

Attracting leads, instead of always chasing after them ... establishing yourself as the go-to authority in your industry ... and spending less money (and effort) to get your message in front of larger audiences.

The map to get you there is in your hands. You just have to use it.

In the remaining pages, you'll find a $145 Copy Critique Certificate to help steer you in the right direction and get one-on-one help. But before giving it to you, I have a favor to ask.

If you found value in what you just read and believe the insight I shared could help another entrepreneur or executive, could you please go back to Amazon.com or wherever you bought this book and leave a review? As you know, reviews help get books in front of new readers.

Of course, after you leave your review, please let me know so I can post your praises (or criticism) on my refrigerator. As with my other books, I'd really like to prove to my wife that I'm doing something useful with all these hours clicking on a keyboard.

Good luck and thank you for sharing your time with me. Please keep me updated on your progress.

Tom Trush
E-mail: tom@writewaysolutions.com
Twitter: @tomtrush
Facebook: http://www.facebook.com/tomtrush

Marketing Tips Review & Resources

- Go beyond what's expected and trust often follows.

- Marketing that matches an expected look and feel goes unnoticed.

- Those who establish trust are the ones who get heard.

- If you want to generate more leads, shine the spotlight away from your company. Stop thinking about what you can get from your marketing and instead focus on what you can give.

- Marketing offers an opportunity to tell stories that your audience can relate to. So share case studies or explain how you helped someone overcome a challenge (preferably one your prospects are experiencing right now).

- Besides their hunger for information, today's prospects are on a continuous quest to find something worth sharing. They seek to distribute activities, opinions and media that entertain or inform.

- When writing a marketing piece, thinking about your needs first creates an instant disconnect. From the opening word to the final punctuation mark, you must focus on how to help your prospects ... how your offer benefits them ... how your product/service makes their lives easier ... and why their lives will be better with what you offer (and more difficult without it).

- If your marketing doesn't provide value, you're just adding contamination in an already tainted marketplace.

- Effective marketing is an evolving process – the amount of change depends on how much work you put forth.

- When you compare your marketing efforts against results achieved by others, you will always fail – at least in your mind. You come up short every time you determine your success by others' accomplishments.

- All good selling is serving.

- Instead of forcing an idea/thought/fact on your prospects, gain an advantage by helping them come to conclusions on their own. Self-tests work well for these situations. You simply walk prospects through questions that prove your knowledge, present a problem and help identify solutions related to your product or service.

- Avoid over-promoting characteristics you should have or actions you're supposed to do.

- Like an artist, your written words are the "paint" that determines what prospects are willing to pay for your product or service.

- To create an alignment, you must match your marketing to your prospects' problems.

- If you wouldn't say something in a one-on-one conversation with a prospect, don't say it in your marketing materials.

- In today's information-driven society, people want to experience what you offer before making a commitment. So anticipate your prospects' desires and be generous with your knowledge.

- Consumers crave information they can believe. They've been exposed to so much aggressive hype, promises and pitches from so-called experts that they're naturally skeptical of self-serving promotion.

- Marketing copy that connects with prospects is conversational. When read aloud, it sounds like you're talking to a friend over lunch.

- Use words that reaffirm people's freedom of choice. In marketing situations, this choice is often whether to buy or not. So you remind prospects that they have the right to decline your offer.

- Difference isn't a characteristic you can just talk about ... you must prove it.

- To achieve the best response, explain what prospects lose by not taking action on your offer. Remind them that their pain and problems continue if they don't get your solution right now.

- People take action on your marketing for their own reasons – not yours.

- Use multiple media formats when creating your content. Sure, almost everyone reads content. But some in your audience may enjoy listening to audio or watching videos too. Furthermore, using different media makes it easier to distribute your content in more places.

- Make your marketing so valuable that prospects would cringe with anxiety if they had to throw it away.

- The best length for marketing materials is whatever you need to properly deliver your marketing message.

- When your product or service – and its marketing – looks like everything else in your industry, you force prospects to use price as the deciding factor when buying.

- When you take an idea they express in their minds and then mention it in your marketing, prospects are likely to agree with what you said. That's why it's critical you match the language your prospects use to describe their situation.

- Positive language creates positive mental conditioning. So if you want prospects to lean toward a "yes" response, put them in a positive state of mind.

- You likely have a list of lost clients that holds hidden profit opportunities. Contact these people now.

- You already established a trust level with past clients. So, logically, it takes less effort to get them to buy again. On the other hand, attracting new clients requires more effort and resources because the trust isn't yet developed.

- Regardless of the medium you use, your best bet when marketing is to test small. Then, once you generate the response you want, invest those profits into larger materials and markets. Any other approach only wastes money.

- Mimic the behavior of influential leaders in your industry.

- The closer you match your prospects' problems, the higher the price they'll pay.

- Companies that consistently generate leads treat marketing as a routine. Distributing a message that attracts prospects and creates clients is done just as much when business booms as when it slows.

- The most effective marketing often doesn't look like marketing.

- You can't market effectively if you rely on interrupting as many people as possible with a message they never asked for.

- Eyeballs don't equal attention.

- "They may forget what you said, but they will never forget how you made them feel."

- In many cases, past customers stop spending only because they aren't given more opportunities to buy.

- You must prove to prospects that they're getting great value – not just a great price. When what you offer becomes indistinguishable from others and clients buy only based on price, your business becomes a commodity.

- There's a purpose for every purchase. And it's this purpose that drives the sale – not the product or service.

- If you run a bad ad, you won't get responses whether you run it 1 or 1,000 times. An ineffective ad can't magically become effective, regardless of how many times you use it.

- One way to temporarily disable your prospects' inner critic is by calling attention to specific problems. After all, problems are "messages" your mind can relate to because you actively think about them.

- When you market in an unconventional manner, you'll feel alone at times. People will criticize you – and that's okay.

$145 Copy Critique Certificate

T his Copy Critique Certificate entitles the possessor to submit any single piece of copy – advertisement, e-mail, postcard, press release, brochure, web page or similar promotional material – for critique by Tom Trush.

_____   _____
Name   Date

Send Copy Critique Certificate, materials and
contact information to Tom at:

tom@writewaysolutions.com (include "Copy Critique" in subject line)
or
fax to 602.606.7920

After personally reviewing your materials, Tom will give you specific recommendations on how to modify your marketing piece for increased responses. You'll get a list of action steps to help position you as an industry authority, deliver higher returns on your marketing investments and allow you to reach larger audiences with less effort.

Terms and Conditions

Copy Critique Certificate expires 12 months from date of purchase. Please allow up to 10 business days for Tom's response. Consultation is delivered by e-mail only. Phone consultations can be scheduled – fees quoted on request. Finished materials or "rough drafts" for planned marketing materials can be submitted. This certificate is only redeemable for listed services.

All copy sent to Tom is kept confidential.

Bibliography

Bly, Robert W. *How to Write & Sell Simple Information for Fun and Profit.* Fresno, CA: Quill Driver Books, 2010

Caples, John. *Tested Advertising Methods.* Paramus, NJ: Prentice Hall, 1997 (5th ed.).

Cialdini, Robert. *Influence: The Psychology of Persuasion.* New York, NY: HarperCollins, 1998.

Collier, Robert. *The Robert Collier Letter Book.* Oak Harbor, WA: Robert Collier Publications, Inc., 1937

Garber, Craig. *How to Make Maximum Money With Minimum Customers.* Lutz, FL: kingofcopy.com, 2009.

Gaudet II, Charles E. *The Predictable Profits Playbook: The Entrepreneur's Guide to Dominating Any Market and Staying on Top.* Telemachus Press, 2014

Glazer, Bill. *Outrageous Advertising That's Outrageously Successful.* New York, NY: Glazer-Kennedy Publishing, 2009.

Hopkins, Claude. *My Life in Advertising.* Lincolnwood, IL: NTC Business Books, 1986, 1966.

Hopkins, Claude. *Scientific Advertising*. Lincolnwood, IL: NTC Business Books, 1986, 1966.

Kennedy, Dan. *No B.S. Direct Marketing*. Entrepreneur Press, 2006.

Lewis, Herschell Gordon. *Direct Mail Copy That Sells!* Englewood Cliffs, NJ: Prentice-Hall, Inc., 1984

Lindstrom, Martin. *Brandwashed: Tricks Companies Use to Manipulate Our Minds and Persuade Us to Buy*. New York, NY: Crown Publishing Group, 2011.

Lorayne, Harry and Lucas, Jerry. *The Memory Book*. New York, NY: Barnes & Noble Books, 1974.

Nicholas, Ted. *Billion Dollar Marketing Secrets: How to Get a Massive Bang for Your Marketing Buck Online and Offline*. Indian Rocks Beach, FL: Ted Nicholas Direct, 2008.

Ogilvy, David. *Ogilvy on Advertising*. New York, NY: Vintage Books, 1983.

Port, Michael. *Book Yourself Solid. The Fastest, Easiest, and Most Reliable System for Getting More Clients Than You Can Handle, Even if You Hate Marketing and Selling*. Hoboken, NJ: John Wiley & Sons, Inc., 2011.

Scott, David Meerman. *The New Rules of Marketing & PR*. Hoboken, NJ: John Wiley & Sons, 2011.

Scott, David Meerman. *Newjacking: How to Inject Your Ideas Into a Breaking News Story and Generate Tons of Media Coverage*. Hoboken, NJ: John Wiley & Sons, 2012.

Simpson, Craig. *The Direct Mail Solution: A Business Owner's Guide to Building a Lead-Generating, Sales-Driving, Money-Making Direct-Mail Campaign*. Entrepreneur Press, 2014

Sugarman, Joe. *The Adweek Copywriting Handbook*. Hoboken, NJ: John Wiley & Sons, 2007.

Whitman, Drew Eric. *Cashvertising: How to Use More Than 100 Secrets of Ad-Agency Psychology to Make Big Money Selling Anything to Anyone*. Franklin Lakes, NJ: Career Press, 2009.

About Tom Trush

As a direct-response copywriter and marketing strategist, Tom Trush helps business owners, entrepreneurs and executives create The "You" Effect™ – a process that transforms ego-based marketing into captivating messages that create customers.

He helps business professionals understand how changing your perspective on prospects can position you as an industry authority, deliver higher returns on your marketing investments and allow you to reach larger audiences with less effort.

In addition to working with clients across the globe, Tom shares his educational approach to marketing at seminars and workshops, as well as in his own information products.

In addition to *Escape the Expected: The Secret Psychology of Selling to Today's Skeptical Consumers*, he is the author of *The "You" Effect: How to Transform Ego-Based Marketing Into Captivating Messages That Create Customers* and *The Reluctant Writer's Guide to Creating Powerful Marketing Materials: 61 Easy Ideas to Attract Prospects and Get More Customers*.

A graduate of Arizona State University, Tom lives in Phoenix, Arizona, with his wife, Michelle, and their two children – Mary and Alex.

Made in the USA
Lexington, KY
02 September 2017